PRISONERS

WITHOUT TRIAL

BOOKS BY ROGER DANIELS

The Politics of Prejudice:
The Anti-Japanese Movement in California and the Struggle
for Japanese Exclusion, 1962; 3rd ed., 1991

The Bonus March: An Episode of the Great Depression, 1971

Concentration Camps, USA: Japanese Americans and WW II, 1971

The Decision to Relocate the Japanese Americans,
1975; 2nd ed., 1983

Concentration Camps, North America:
Japanese Americans and Canadians during WW II, 1981

Asian America: Chinese and Japanese
in the United States since 1850, 1988

Coming to America: A History of Immigration
and Ethnicity in American Life, 1990; 2nd ed., 2002

Not Like Us: Immigrants and Minorities in America, 1890–1924, 1997

American Immigration: A Student Companion, 2001

Guarding the Golden Door:
American Immigration Policy and Immigrants
Since 1882, 2004

[with Harry H. L. Kitano]:
American Racism: Exploration of the Nature of Prejudice, 1970

Asian Americans: Emerging Minorities, 1988; 3rd ed., 2001

[with Otis L. Graham]:
Debating American Immigration, 1882–Present, 2001

[with Sandra C. Taylor and Harry H. L. Kitano]:
Japanese Americans: From Relocation to Redress,
1986; 2nd ed., 1991

[ed.] *American Concentration Camps:*
A Documentary History of the Relocation and Incarceration
of Japanese Americans, 1941–1945, 9 vols., 1989

PRISONERS WITHOUT TRIAL

Japanese Americans in World War II

REVISED EDITION

ROGER

DANIELS

A CRITICAL ISSUE

CONSULTING EDITOR: ERIC FONER

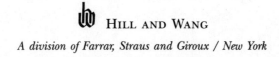 HILL AND WANG

A division of Farrar, Straus and Giroux / New York

Hill and Wang
A division of Farrar, Straus and Giroux
18 West 18th Street, New York 10011

LIBRARY OF CONGRESS CATALOGING-IN-PUBLICATION DATA
Daniels, Roger.
    Prisoners without trial : Japanese Americans in World War II /
Roger Daniels.— Rev. ed.
        p.   cm.— (A critical issue)
    Includes bibliographical references and index.
    ISBN-13: 978-0-8090-7896-7
    ISBN-10: 0-8090-7896-1
    1. Japanese Americans—Evacuation and relocation, 1942–1945.
2. Japanese Americans—Pacific States—History—20th century.
3. World War, 1939–1945—United States.   I. Title. II. Series.

D769.8.A6D37 2004
940.53'089'956073—dc22

                                          2004047328

Designed by Fritz Metsch

www.fsgbooks.com

11   13   15   14   12   10

FOR MY GRANDSON,
CONNOR JUSTIN ARMSTRONG DANIELS,
B. FEBRUARY 19, 2003,
WITH LOVE AND HIGH HOPES

CONTENTS

PREFACE

Since I have written extensively about what their own government did to Japanese Americans during World War II, I have not thought it necessary to document this work as fully as its predecessors, especially since hundreds of relevant documents have been published in the nine-volume set *American Concentration Camps* (1989). This book differs from my previous work in two ways: it is briefer, and it is the first such account to be written after the enactment and execution of what the Japanese Americans call redress, the apology and token monetary compensation voted by Congress in 1988.

The intellectual debts piled up in the course of writing even a brief book are large, and only the most pressing can be acknowledged here. Eric Foner, the consulting editor of this series, and Arthur Wang, its publisher, each read the manuscript and had valuable criticisms and suggestions, as did a fellow student of the Japanese American experience, Dr. Louis Fiset. I wrote this book while visiting at two institutions during a year of leave. Evelyn Sobremonte and Laurie Dellemonache at the University of Calgary and Renate Guggenberger and Maria Meth at the University of Innsbruck went out of their way to help a visitor. My leaves were supported by Gene Lewis, the head of the University of Cincinnati's History Department, and Joseph A. Caruso, dean of the McMicken College of Arts and Sciences. Special thanks are due also to my colleague, Bruce Levine, and, as always and most important, to my wife, Judith M. Daniels, who listened, read, commented, corrected, and questioned on two continents.

ROGER DANIELS
Calgary–Innsbruck, 1991–2

PREFACE TO THE REVISED EDITION

In doing this edition I have accumulated new debts that must be acknowledged. Two professionals with the National Park Service, Alisa Lynch, Chief of Interpretation and Cultural Resources Management at the Manzanar National Historic Site, and Dwight Pitcaithley, the Park Service's chief historian, were extremely helpful. Alisa went to great lengths in supplying facts and images, while my old friend Dwight gave me good advice, as usual. Heather Register, of the University of Arkansas–Little Rock, hunted down and provided images, while my colleagues David Stradling, in Cincinnati, and Louis Fiset, in Seattle, and my former student Allan W. Austin, gave information and counsel.

At Hill and Wang, my publisher, Thomas LeBien, who in suggesting doing this edition, again demonstrated rare skill in editing without intruding; Kristina McGowan was a facilitator par excellence; and thanks also to copyeditor Sybil Pincus and cover designer Lynn Buckley. Again, of course, I thank Judith, who has been my literary conscience for more than four decades.

RD
Cincinnati, 2004

PRISONERS
WITHOUT TRIAL

BACKGROUND FOR A
ROUNDUP, 1850–1941

THIS book will describe and attempt to explain how and why nearly 120,000 Japanese Americans were taken from their homes in the spring and early summer of 1942 and incarcerated in concentration camps by the United States government. The United States was then at war with the Empire of Japan and its violation of civil and human rights was justified by President Franklin D. Roosevelt on the grounds of military necessity. These men, women, and children, more than two-thirds of them American citizens, were exiled from their homes and put into desolate camps simply because they or their parents had been born in Japan. Once characterized as "our worst wartime mistake," this was neither a mistake nor an error in judgment nor an inadvertence. The wartime abuse of Japanese Americans, it is now clear, was merely a link in a chain of racism that stretched back to the earliest contacts between Asians and whites on American soil. A 1981 report by the Presidential Commission on the Wartime Relocation and Internment of Civilians put it nicely, concluding that the relocation and incarceration of the Japanese Americans

> was not justified by military necessity, and the decisions which followed from it . . . were not driven by analysis of military conditions. The broad historical causes which shaped these decisions were race prejudice, war hysteria, and a failure of political leadership . . . A grave injustice was done to American citizens and resident aliens of Japanese ancestry who, without individual review or any pro-

bative evidence against them, were excluded, removed and detained by the United States during World War II.

To understand these unprecedented and now almost universally regretted wartime actions, it is necessary to look beyond the war years and beyond even the earliest arrival of Japanese immigrants in America and examine, however briefly, the Chinese, who were the first large group of immigrants from Asia, and the reception they received. The experience of the Chinese in nineteenth-century America served in many ways as a kind of rehearsal for what would happen to later immigrants from Asia.

This is not to say that all immigrants from Asia were alike. There are many differences between Asian ethnic groups and, for that matter, there are great differences within Asian ethnic groups. But to most Americans in the late nineteenth and early twentieth century, all Asian immigrants seemed alike and alike seemed to present a threat to the American standard of living and to the racial integrity of the nation. These attitudes and the actions that accompanied them were clearly racist, but most Americans in those years would not have recognized them as such. They would have argued that their attitudes were simply "American." There is more than a little logic in such an argument, because the United States was then an explicitly racist nation which discriminated in both law and custom against any persons who were not recognized as "white." In fact, many "white" ethnic groups also suffered severe discrimination, but discrimination that was customary rather than statutory. The treatment of Asians in America was related to the dispossession of Native Americans, the enslavement of African Americans, and the maltreatment of Mexican Americans, Catholics, Jews, and others.

Although a few Asians, mostly seamen, had come to the Eastern United States in the late eighteenth century, the immigration of Asians in significant numbers dates from 1850, when Chinese men began to arrive in San Francisco. Almost all of them were attracted by the gold that had been discovered outside Sacramento, a little over a hundred miles away. The Chinese became a small part of a massive migration, the first

TABLE 1

CHINESE IMMIGRATION AND POPULATION, 1860–1880

Immigration of Chinese to the United States

YEARS	NO. OF IMMIGRANTS
To 1860	41,443
1861–1870	64,301
1871–1880	123,823
Total	229,567

Chinese American Population by Census

YEAR	UNITED STATES	PACIFIC STATES	CALIFORNIA
1860	34,933	n/a	34,933
1870	63,199	52,841	49,277
1880	104,468	87,828	75,132

Source: U.S. Immigration and Census data

great American Gold Rush, which in a matter of months brought more than a hundred thousand newcomers into the sleepy former Mexican province. Most of the newcomers were Americans from the "states," but there were large numbers of Europeans and Latin Americans, and a few Australians as well as Chinese. Gold drew them all—the Chinese characters for "California" can also be translated as "golden mountain"—but from the first the Asians and the Latin Americans, although tolerated, were not treated equally.

It is clear from the data that a great many of the nearly 250,000 Chinese who came to the United States before 1880 eventually returned to China. (Table 1 shows early Chinese immigration and population.) It is a common practice among most immigrant groups throughout American history for single males to come to make some money and then return home "rich" men. Such persons are called "sojourners," as opposed to those who come planning to stay. A man who could bring back $400 to China was considered "rich"; he could buy some land or get his family out of debt. According to mid-century American consular reports from the China coast, some actually managed to do so. But immigrants' plans do not always work out: sojourners of many nationalities become settlers, and many who plan to settle return home.

Racism and other forms of prejudice were entrenched in the United States when the Chinese began to arrive. Early in their colonial history, Americans had learned to despise the Native Americans and to regard blacks, whether slave or free, as inherently inferior beings. Later, hostile contact with Mexicans, first in Texas and then throughout the Southwest, added the Mexicans to the list of inferiors—a list that expanded to include all Latin Americans after large numbers of Chileans and other Latins emigrated to California. The great nineteenth-century American philosopher Josiah Royce, a native Californian, understood the phenomenon well and commented on it with savage irony:

> The life of a Spanish American in the mines in the early days, if frequently profitable, was apt to be a little disagreeable. It served him right of course. He had no business, as an alien, to come to the land God had given us. And if he was a native Californian, or "greaser," then so much the worse for him. He was so much more our born foe; we hated his whole degenerate, thieving, landowning, lazy and discontented race. Some of them were now even bandits; most of them by this time were, with our help, more or less drunkards; and it was not our fault if they were not all rascals! So they deserved no better.

Given this harsh climate of opinion, it is hardly surprising that the Chinese were badly treated, first in California and then elsewhere in the West. California's first legal code in 1850 barred the testimony of blacks and Indians against whites, and the California courts soon barred the Chinese as well. This, in effect, gave criminals a license to steal from Chinese miners, who generally lived in isolated ethnic enclaves near the diggings, as California's early mines were called. It is no wonder that the phrase "a Chinaman's chance" came to mean no chance at all. Although many of the early Chinese immigrants, like most immigrants in the Gold Rush era, headed for the diggings, European American miners often drove them and Latin American miners away. In addition, the legislature passed a "foreign miner's tax," the first of many discriminatory statutes aimed at the Chinese.

In the face of prejudice and abuse, which included frequent assaults and occasional murders, for which whites were almost never punished, the Chinese continued to come to California and the American West. Despite everything, it was possible for the Chinese to earn much more in America than in China. The labor of Chinese workers and entrepreneurs contributed significantly to the economic growth of the American West in both industry and agriculture. Their most spectacular contribution was building the Western leg of the first transcontinental railroad. When that road was completed, in May 1869, some ten thousand Chinese railroad workers were laid off. Most of them went to San Francisco, where their presence triggered the most violent phase of organized anti-Chinese agitation.

A powerful movement of workingmen who resented Chinese competition developed. Led by a recent Irish immigrant, Dennis Kearney, it had as its slogan "The Chinese Must Go!" Its real goal was an end to Chinese immigration. Most Western politicians soon found it prudent to support the movement, even though many of them, such as the railroad magnate Leland Stanford, continued to employ Chinese labor. Laboring men and their organizations throughout the nation backed the Westerners' demands in 1870 after a few Chinese were hired as strikebreakers in the Eastern United States. In 1882 Congress passed and President Chester A. Arthur signed the Chinese Exclusion Act, which barred further immigration of Chinese laborers—but not all Chinese—for ten years. This law was extended for ten more years in 1892 and was made permanent in 1902. The 1882 act was the first federal law to discriminate against any immigrant group and thus set an important precedent.

It was only after Chinese immigration had been stopped that statistically significant Japanese immigration began, although a few Japanese had come to the United States just after the Civil War. Table 2 shows the growth of the ethnic Japanese population in the United States.

To keep these figures in perspective, it must be remembered

TABLE 2

JAPANESE IMMIGRATION AND POPULATION, 1890–1940
Immigration of Japanese to the United States

YEARS	NO. OF IMMIGRANTS
To 1890	3,000
1891–1900	27,000
1901–1908	127,000
1909–1924	118,000
Total	275,000

Japanese American Population by Census

YEAR	JAPANESE IN UNITED STATES	JAPANESE ON PACIFIC COAST	JAPANESE IN CALIFORNIA
1900	24,326	18,629	10,151
1910	72,157	57,703	41,356
1920	111,010	94,490	71,952
1930	138,834	119,893	97,456
1940	126,948	112,353	93,717

Source: U.S. Immigration and Census data
Japanese in the Hawaiian Islands are not included

that between 1900 and 1940 the population of the United States grew from 76 million to 130 million and that ethnic Japanese never constituted as much as two-tenths of one percent (0.02%) of the total population or more than two and one-tenth percent (2.1%) of California's population. Looking at these figures rationally, one finds it difficult to see how Japanese Americans could have seemed a threat to the nation, but racial fears are more often based on fantasy than on reality.

Initially, Japanese immigration followed the pattern of Chinese immigration and that of many other groups of the time. Most immigrants were young adult males who came intending to sojourn, although, almost from the beginning, there were some who intended to make America their home. As the first groups of newcomers from the land of the rising sun arrived, an anti-Japanese movement developed, first in California and then elsewhere in the West. Its organizers saw in the Japanese the same "threat" as in the Chinese. Given the racial climate in the United States, it seems clear that if Japan had been as weak a nation as China was in those years, a Japanese Exclusion Act on the Chinese model would have been passed by Congress easily.

But Japan was not a weak nation. Japan was victorious in the Russo–Japanese War of 1904–5. It was not only the most powerful Asian nation but also well on the road to becoming a world power. In present-day language, Japan was the first country to move from the Third World to the First. Japan's autocratic rulers were not really interested in the lives and welfare of a few hundred thousand of its peasants overseas, but they were convinced that if they allowed Japanese people to be mistreated abroad—as most Asian emigrants were—it would be detrimental to Japan's new status as a world power. Farsighted American leaders, such as Theodore Roosevelt, were aware of Japan's growing strength and acted to inhibit anti-Japanese legislation. Thus, early in the twentieth century, Japan's power served to protect the status of its emigrants. Tokyo, in collaboration with Washington, was able to frustrate the anti-Japanese movement for two decades.

That movement, like the anti-Chinese movement, was begun by labor leaders; in fact, Dennis Kearney lived long enough to be one of its pioneers, in 1892. But there were too few Japanese in California for many people to take much notice. Eight years later, the anti-Japanese crusade really took off, and took off from a broader base than its predecessor. Middle-class politicians, particularly those commonly styled "progressive," were instrumental in the movement's growth and success. The first sign of this was a speech by San Francisco's millionaire reform mayor, James Duval Phelan. Appearing at a rally called to urge Congress to renew the Chinese Exclusion Act, the mayor noted a new danger:

The Japanese are starting the same tide of immigration which we thought we had checked twenty years ago . . . The Chinese and Japanese are not bona fide citizens. They are not the stuff of which American citizens can be made

. . . Personally we have nothing against the Japanese, but as they will not assimilate with us and their social life is so different from ours, let them keep a respectful distance.

The three major California political parties—Republican, Democrat, and Populist—took a stand against all Asiatic immigration in 1900, as did the national American Federation of Labor, but the anti-Japanese movement did not have an impact beyond the Far West until 1905. That February, the conservative San Francisco *Chronicle*, then the most influential newspaper on the Pacific Coast, ran a sensational series of articles. Beginning with a front-page headline, THE JAPANESE INVASION, THE PROBLEM OF THE HOUR, the paper added new elements to the old economic and cultural arguments against Asians: sex and intrigue. It maintained that Japanese men were a menace to white women, that every immigrant was "a Japanese spy," and it claimed, with wild inaccuracy, that there were at least 100,000 of the "little brown men" in the country. The inflammatory articles continued almost daily for months and were much copied and discussed up and down the Pacific Coast. Typical headlines read:

CRIME AND POVERTY GO HAND IN HAND WITH ASIATIC LABOR
HOW JAPANESE IMMIGRATION COMPANIES OVERRIDE LAWS
BROWN MEN ARE MADE CITIZENS ILLEGALLY
JAPANESE A MENACE TO AMERICAN WOMEN
BROWN MEN AN EVIL IN THE PUBLIC SCHOOLS
ADULT JAPANESE CROWD OUT CHILDREN
THE YELLOW PERIL—HOW JAPANESE CROWD OUT THE WHITE RACE
BROWN PERIL ASSUMES NATIONAL PROPORTIONS
BROWN ARTISANS STEAL BRAINS OF WHITES

The month after the *Chronicle* series began, California politicians took up the anti-Japanese crusade. Both houses of the state legislature unanimously adopted an insulting anti-Japanese resolution which echoed the paper's diatribes. The immigrants were denounced as "undesirable," as not wishing "to assimilate with our people or to become Americans," as "mere transients [who] do not buy land . . . a blight on the [state's] prosperity." The resolution concluded with a vision of worse things to come:

The close of the war between Japan and Russia will surely bring to our shores hordes, to be counted only in thousands, of the discharged soldiers of the Japanese Army, who will crowd the State with immoral, intemperate, quarrelsome men, bound to labor for a pittance, and to subsist on a supply with which a white man can hardly sustain life.

The legislators were woefully ignorant of what was really happening in their state: within a few years, their chief complaints would center on Japanese purchases of land. However, if California had been an independent republic, it would quickly have put an end to Japanese immigration. But it was part of a federal union. This placed limitations on the ability of California to wage "war" on the Japanese.

Although the Constitution says nothing about immigration—save for the clause about the slave trade (Art. I, Sec. 9)—the Founding Fathers clearly assumed that immigration would continue, as they empowered Congress "to establish a uniform rule of naturalization" (Art. I, Sec. 8) and provided that only "a natural-born citizen" could become President or Vice-President (Art. II, Sec. 1). In 1790 Congress adopted the first naturalization statute, which limited that right to "free white persons." Although Congress would pass no legislation regulating immigration until the 1870s, the Supreme Court ruled, in the Passenger Cases of 1849, that no state could regulate immigration. The court defined immigration as "foreign commerce," which was one of the enumerated powers of Congress (Art. I, Sec. 8). The Thirteenth and Fourteenth Amendments, adopted in 1865 and 1868 to protect the rights of blacks, abolished slavery and created a national citizenship by making "all persons born or naturalized in the United States" citizens of the nation *and* "of the State wherein they reside." Consequently, the 1790 naturalization law needed to be rewritten.

Since slavery had been abolished, the word "free" became redundant and was dropped. In addition, in 1870 the Reconstruction Congress, still determined to protect the freedmen, added the words "and persons of African descent" to the phrase "white persons" already in the statute. A few in Congress wanted to make naturalization color-blind, but organized opposition to

Chinese immigration made that impossible. Thus, unlike white and black immigrants, immigrants from Asia could not become naturalized citizens, and remained "aliens ineligible to citizenship." But, thanks to the Fourteenth Amendment, any of their children born in the United States (and later in the Territory of Hawaii) were citizens like every other native-born person.

This being the case, the California legislature and California cities and counties could harass resident Japanese but could neither expel those who were already there nor prevent others from moving in. This harassment brought California into conflict with the executive branch of the federal government, which wanted to keep on reasonably good terms with Japan. The first significant clash involved not laborers, or even farmers, but schoolchildren.

Not surprisingly, California law had long allowed "separate schools for children of Chinese or Mongolian descent," and San Francisco had established a segregated school for Chinese pupils in the 1870s. Since 1893 its school board had periodically discussed requiring Japanese children to go to the school in Chinatown, but only on October 11, 1906, did the local officials formally order them to do so. The order went unnoticed in most of America until some days later, when a Tokyo newspaper printed a garbled version of it, and what is usually called "the San Francisco School Board affair" escalated into an international incident. President Theodore Roosevelt, who had signed the latest renewal of the Chinese Exclusion Act and who, we now know, privately felt that the Japanese were also "undesirable immigrants," publicly attacked discrimination against Japanese pupils, in his 1906 State of the Union message, as a "wicked absurdity." What concerned him were not abstract principles of justice but reasons of state: "the mob of a single city," he told Congress, could "plunge us into war."

Roosevelt initiated the long process of "settling" the question of Japanese immigration; the school-board issue was but the tip of the iceberg. Segregation by race was perfectly legal, so the President had to resort to persuasion and negotiation. He called California congressmen to the White House and eventually brought some San Francisco leaders there, too. He got them to withdraw the segregation order, with a combination of threats and promises that he would put a stop to Japanese immigration. In collaboration with the Republican governor of California, Roosevelt persuaded the legislature not to take anti-Japanese actions. In fact, Republican governors of California "sat upon the lid" of this issue, as one of them put it, until 1913. Roosevelt then began negotiations with Japan which resulted in the Gentlemen's Agreement, a series of notes exchanged between the governments in 1907–8. Japan agreed to stop issuing passports to Japanese laborers to come to the United States, and the Americans promised not to legislate against Japanese, which saved Japanese "face." It was also agreed that divided Japanese families in the United States could be reunited, a provision which led to results undreamed of by the negotiators. There was a good deal of hypocrisy on both sides. Roosevelt pretended that he believed in racial equality; the Japanese studiously ignored the existence of segregated schools for Japanese in four small Sacramento County school districts where Japanese pupils were an absolute majority.

The Gentlemen's Agreement eased tensions about the presence of Japanese in the American West, but it did not resolve them; in some ways, it made them worse. Under the Gentlemen's Agreement, tens of thousands of Japanese women, and some children, legally immigrated to the United States between 1908 and 1924 as family members of established Japanese residents. Some of the men had left wives behind; others got married and brought their wives across the Pacific. Some of these wives were "picture brides," women who were married by proxy in Japan and came to join husbands they had never seen. This practice, unfamiliar to most Americans, led many Californians and others in the Far West to believe that there was a conspiracy between Washington and Tokyo to flood the Pacific Coast with Japanese.

Then a new anti-Japanese controversy broke out, this one over the ownership of agricultural land by persons born in Japan, who could not, we must remember, become citizens. By 1909, Japanese farmers in California controlled nearly 150,000 acres of farmland. Ten years later the figure was some 450,000 acres. This was about one percent of California's agricultural land, but because of the labor-intensive nature of Japanese American agriculture, those crops represented about 10 percent

($67 million) of the value of California's harvest. In 1913 the California legislature considered an alien land bill to deny "aliens ineligible to citizenship"—that is, persons of Asian ethnicity born in Asia—the right to own agricultural land. (Japanese could own urban real estate because that right was protected by a Japanese American commercial treaty.) Similar bills had been throttled in previous years, but in 1913 the political situation was different: Woodrow Wilson, a Democrat, was now in the White House. California's progressive Republican governor, Hiram W. Johnson, had been Theodore Roosevelt's Vice-Presidential running mate in their unsuccessful 1912 race for the White House against Wilson and conservative Republican William Howard Taft. Whereas in 1911 Johnson had, however reluctantly, cooperated with a Republican Administration in thwarting anti-Japanese legislative action, now he helped to draft the offensive legislation. Despite appeals for restraint from the Wilson Administration—Secretary of State William Jennings Bryan made a dramatic visit to Sacramento to address the legislature—California enacted an alien land law in 1913. Other states in the Far West soon followed suit.

Again, a great deal of hypocrisy was involved. Wilson and his allies were even more racially biased than most Republicans and had actually attacked Roosevelt as being soft on "Japs" in the 1912 campaign. And Johnson knew, as his private correspondence reveals, that the alien land law would be ineffective: even though it prohibited outright ownership, it permitted both leasing and share-cropping contracts. This deliberate loophole—it was to the advantage of white landowners to be able to lease land to the Japanese—was plugged by a 1920 alien land law, but there were other legal methods by which Japanese farmers could evade the laws. Well-to-do farmers like the millionaire "potato baron" George Shima could hire lawyers to form corporations for them which could hold land while the Japanese held the stock. Farmers with American-born children had an even simpler expedient: they could put their land in their children's names, even if the children were infants, and, as legal guardians of their children, they would retain control of the land. The result of the legislative actions, and of diplomatic actions, was to increase tension and heighten feelings about Japanese conspiracies against America in general and against California and the Far West in particular.

The final episodes in the struggles over the restriction of Japanese immigration and influence came in the early 1920s, a period of intense nationalism that John Higham has labeled "the tribal twenties." Japanese American tensions had been further exacerbated after the First World War by Japan's aggressiveness as exemplified by the notorious Twenty-one Demands, which aimed to establish Japanese hegemony over China. Tokyo, still trying to save face, attempted to achieve a kind of détente. It sacrificed the interests of its immigrants in America by modifying the rules under which Japanese women could get passports for the United States: brides could no longer come unless an actual, as opposed to a proxy, marriage had taken place. Although what Japan feared most—a Japanese Exclusion Act modeled on the 1882 anti-Chinese law—was never enacted, the United States achieved the same result in the general Immigration Act of 1924.

That act, a drastic and biased curtailment of immigration directed essentially against Southern and Eastern Europeans, set up quotas for each nation based on the number of its immigrants who had been recorded as living in the United States in the 1890 census. Had Japan's quota been set on the same basis as those for other nations, as the bill originally provided, its quota would have been the minimum—just a hundred persons per year—although some close relatives of residents would have been allowed in, too. But Congress, over the feeble protests of Secretary of State Charles Evans Hughes —President Calvin Coolidge was opposed but remained silent —amended the bill to bar all "aliens ineligible to citizenship." Japan got her quota, but no Japanese person could use it!

Thus ended the legal and diplomatic controversies over immigration and the rights of resident Japanese in the United States. In Japan there were mass protests against what was correctly regarded as a deliberate insult. Apart from the inherent injustice of the treatment meted out to the Japanese in the United States, these events were an essential part of what George

TABLE 3

ETHNIC JAPANESE, BY GENERATION, 1920–1940

YEAR	TOTAL POPULATION	FOREIGN-BORN	U.S.-BORN	PERCENT U.S.-BORN
1920	111,010	81,502	29,508	26.6
1930	138,834	70,477	68,357	49.2
1940	126,947	47,305	79,642	62.7

Source: U.S. Census data

F. Kennan has called the "long and unhappy story" of U.S.–Japanese relations in the decades before the Great Pacific War of 1941–45.

The ending of immigration from Japan did not end the growth of the Japanese community in the United States. The total population did shrink as a significant number of Issei (the first or immigrant generation) returned to Japan. But there was rapid growth in the second, or Nisei, generation, and by 1940 it outnumbered its parents, so that a small but thriving ethnic community was established. Table 3 shows the growth of that generation.

In 1940 the Japanese American community was heavily concentrated in the Pacific states, where nearly 113,000 (88.5%) lived: most of them, 94,000, lived in California; 15,000 in Washington State; and the remaining 4,000 in Oregon. Only three other states—Colorado, New York, and Utah—had as many as a thousand Japanese. Even within the Pacific states, Nikkei (ethnic Japanese) were heavily concentrated: Los Angeles County had 37,000; King and Pierce counties (Seattle and Tacoma) had more than 11,000; and another 11,000 lived in three San Francisco Bay area counties.

Japanese employment was also highly concentrated: in 1940, just over half (51.4%) of all employed Japanese males worked in agriculture, forestry, or fishing, as did a third of employed Japanese females. Almost a quarter (23.6%) of all Japanese worked in the wholesale and retail trade, while more than a sixth (17.1%) were servants or performed other personal services. These three sectors employed seven-eighths of the Japanese labor force. Few Japanese Americans were employed in manufacturing, transportation, communications, the professions, or government service. A large proportion of those in retail and wholesale worked in Japanese-owned businesses, many of which were an extension of the ethnic agricultural economy. There were many Japanese enterprises in the large City Market in Los Angeles, which sold fruits and vegetables grown by Japanese farmers. While most Japanese businesses there were small fruit-and-vegetable stands, a few of the larger Japanese produce houses grossed $1 million or more annually. At the wholesale level, the total volume of Japanese business in Los Angeles was estimated at $25 million in 1940. In addition, many Japanese did contract gardening there and in other West Coast cities.

Japanese entrepreneurs found many niches in the service sector. A private 1935 survey of Japanese businesses in Seattle listed 183 hotels, 148 grocery stores, 94 dye works (dry cleaners), 64 market stands, 57 produce houses, 42 gardeners, 36 restaurants, 36 barbershops, and 21 laundries. The high concentration in hotels—which catered to workingmen—was a phenomenon peculiar to the Seattle Japanese. Some of these businesses dealt almost exclusively with the ethnic community, but most served the entire population. Similar lists could be drawn up for the other cities with significant concentrations of Japanese.

But the heart of the Japanese American economy was in the country. Unlike most immigrant groups since the Civil War, which have been heavily concentrated in cities, the Japanese were concentrated in rural areas. The U.S. census in 1940 counted more than 6,000 Japanese-operated farms on the Pacific Coast; Issei farmers tilled more than 250,000 acres, whose total value was $72.6 million. The average farm was small, a little over forty acres; most were family enterprises which specialized in growing fruits and vegetables.

Anti-Japanese propagandists argued that the Issei farmers had driven out white farmers, but this was not the case. In many instances, the Japanese opened up new lands with their labor-intensive, high-yield agriculture, which contrasted with resource-intensive, low-yield American agriculture. Japanese farmers supplemented rather than competed with other Far Western farmers. Their food production helped make possible the dramatic growth of the population on the Pacific Coast, from 2.4 million in 1900 to 9.7 million in 1940.

As the census data suggest, the Japanese-American community had become predominantly lower middle class within one generation. Although there were Japanese individuals and families below the poverty line, first-generation families owned real property—farms and businesses—to a much greater degree than did the general American population. The industry and frugality of the Issei were acknowledged by their friends, their enemies, and, perhaps most of all, by their overworked and underpaid offspring. The Issei generation, like so many immigrant generations before and since, tried to re-create the world it had left behind. Since American society made every effort to keep the Issei segregated, they were probably less exposed to some aspects of Americanization than were most other contemporaneous immigrant groups. Trade unions and professional associations barred them from membership, so they had to form their own. American law denied Issei the right to become naturalized citizens, so they could not become voters. The newspapers and magazines they read were in Japanese, and the Japanese American press took most of its foreign news from Domei, the Japanese government-controlled news agency. If Japanese Americans attended a Buddhist temple, the priest was subsidized by the Japanese government; most of the increasing number who adopted Christianity attended segregated services in domestic mission churches whose pastors were most often either former missionaries or converts from Japan.

Even more than most immigrants, the Issei generation lived, worked, and prayed in an ethnic enclave, largely cut off from meaningful contact with most other Americans. But their children, the Nisei generation, like most of the children of immigrant America, were exposed to the acculturating influences of public schools. These influences were probably stronger on Nisei than on most immigrant children of that era, because they stayed in school longer and were more likely to graduate and to go on to college or other post-secondary education than were children of most other immigrant groups. From almost the very beginning of the Japanese American experience, the institutions of the ethnic community placed great stress on education.

Nisei children were urged not only to attend schools but to excel. All the studies of Japanese American students—beginning with several done at Stanford University in the 1920s and 1930s—show that, in both attitude and achievement, Nisei pupils were well above the norm. A study of truancy in Los Angeles for the 1930s reported that only one truant in ten thousand was a Japanese, and a history of Seattle noted that Nisei won academic honors "out of all proportion to their numbers." In 1937, for example, three Nisei were valedictorians and two salutatorians in the city's nine high schools. The comments of a San Pedro, California, fisherman to his son, while somewhat exaggerated, nicely epitomize the attitude of a whole generation:

If you graduate from college, I will proudly meet our ancestors in heaven . . . Continue with American higher education . . . show the Americans your ability . . . that is your duty to your parents.

Most Nisei fulfilled their duties to their parents by doing well in school, but it became increasingly apparent to many of them that their education was wasted. Many graduated only to become workers in a family business or farm. Some managed to get white-collar government jobs by scoring high in civil-service exams: several hundred had such jobs in California by early 1942. But the school systems in which they had excelled simply would not—or perhaps could not—hire them, even though relatively large numbers of Japanese Americans were trained as teachers. In Los Angeles, for example, not one Japanese American teacher was hired until after World War II. White parents, it was argued, would complain if a Japanese American teacher were in charge of their children.

Many of the Issei were rightfully proud of their accomplishments in the face of great obstacles, but the young Japanese Americans lived on the horns of what John Modell has called the "Nisei dilemma." As he describes it:

[The Nisei] had inherited from [their] parents a remarkable desire to succeed in the face of hardship, but had also learned the American definition of success, by which standard the accommodation made by his parents could not be considered satisfactory.

By 1940 the oldest Nisei were adults with children of their own: the census numbers included some five thousand Sansei, or third-generation Japanese Americans. Most Nisei, however, were much younger: the median age of Japanese American citizens in 1942 was twenty-one years. The older Nisei had tried, without much success, to break out of the ethnic enclaves in which their parents had made a relatively comfortable accommodation. They tried to enter mainstream politics by forming Nisei Young Republican and Young Democratic clubs, but without significant result, although a few did run, unsuccessfully, for political office. The major organization of the Nisei, the Japanese American Citizens League (JACL)—what we would call today a civil-rights organization—sought to disassociate the whole second generation from its parents by barring the Issei from membership because they were not American citizens. The JACL tried to surmount not just the Nisei dilemma but the whole Japanese American dilemma: how to avoid identification with Japan when one has a Japanese face. Its official creed, still in use, was written in 1940 by JACL official Mike Masaoka, as tensions between the United States and Japan escalated. It is an attempt to demonstrate loyalty. The creed's superpatriotism and its optimism in the face of discrimination are easy to disparage, but behind its blandness lay desperation. The creed proclaimed:

I am proud that I am an American citizen of Japanese ancestry, for my very background makes me appreciate more fully the wonderful advantages of this nation. I believe in her institutions, ideals and traditions; I glory in her heritage; I boast of her history; I trust in her future. She has granted me liberties and opportunities such as no individual enjoys in this world today. She has given me an education befitting kings. She has entrusted me with the responsibilities of the franchise. She has permitted me to build a home, to earn a livelihood, to worship, think, speak and act as I please—as a free man equal to every other man.

Although some individuals may discriminate against me, I shall never become bitter or lose faith, for I know that such persons are not representative of the American people. True, I shall do all in my power to discourage such practices, but I shall do it in the American way—above board, in the open, through courts of law, by education, by proving myself to be worthy of equal treatment and consideration. I am firm in my belief that American sportsmanship and attitude of fair play will judge citizenship and patriotism on the basis of action and achievement, and not on the basis of physical characteristics. Because I believe in America, and I trust she believes in me, and because I have received innumerable benefits from her, I pledge myself to do honor to her at all times and all places; to support her constitution; to obey her laws; to respect her flag; to defend her against all enemies, foreign and domestic; to actively assume my duties and obligations as a citizen, cheerfully and without any reservations whatsoever, in the hope that I may become a better American in a greater America.

The creed downplayed racism and pretended that discrimination came from a few individuals. Within two years of the time it was written, most mainland Japanese Americans were behind barbed wire and American society from top to bottom was permeated by more vicious racism against Japanese Americans than ever before. The pious, patriotic platitudes of the JACL had availed Japanese Americans little: most Americans could only remember that their ancestors came from the country that had bombed Pearl Harbor.

2

THE POLITICS OF

INCARCERATION, 1941–1942

T HE attack on Pearl Harbor shortly after sunrise on Sunday, December 7, 1941, by planes of the Imperial Japanese Navy was both a surprise and not a surprise. The attack was certainly a tactical surprise: it caught the sleepy American forces unprepared despite formal warnings from Washington.* The Japanese aviators sank or damaged nineteen ships of the United States Navy and killed some 2,300 Americans. But that Japan and America went to war was not a surprise. Such a war had been anticipated for decades, sometimes eagerly, by military leaders of both countries. In Japan, at least one major leader, Admiral Isoroku Yamamoto, the man who planned the Pearl Harbor attack, was not sanguine about the outcome of a Japanese American war. He wrote that, given surprise, Japan could "run wild for six months or a year," but after that time he had no confidence. His doubts were not shared by most Japanese military leaders.

American military leaders were also confident before hostilities began. Japan, coded "Orange" in the "Rainbow Plans" of the American armed forces, had long been "the most probable enemy"—at least as far as the United States Navy was concerned. Many political leaders also foresaw the coming of war. Twenty-one years earlier, in far-away Moscow, Lenin had predicted:

* Much has been written about Pearl Harbor, a great deal of it containing unsubstantiated sensational claims that President Roosevelt knew that the attack was coming, etc. The best brief refutation of this is a review of John Toland's book, *Infamy*, by the distinguished American historian of Japan, Robert J. C. Butow, in the *Journal of Japanese Studies*, 1983.

War is brewing between [Japan and America]. They cannot live in peace on the shores of the Pacific, although those shores are three thousand versts apart . . . There is a vast literature devoted to the future Japanese-American war. That war is brewing, that war is inevitable, is beyond doubt.

Much of the "vast literature" the Soviet leader referred to was fiction, a large portion of it of the so-called yellow-peril variety, depicting the invasion of the United States by an Asian power, usually Japan. Dozens of American short stories, books, and motion pictures played variations on this theme, and, as John Dower has shown in *War Without Mercy*, a similar literature existed in Japan.

If this was the case, why were Americans shocked when war did come? They were shocked because they simply had not imagined that Japan had either the capacity or the daring to execute successfully an operation as difficult as the raid on Pearl Harbor. That Americans consistently underestimated Japanese capacities, before, during, and after World War II, was a corollary of the racism which assumed that white brains and power were always better than those of people of color.

Japanese Americans were also surprised and yet not surprised by the coming of war. Many of the older members of the Nisei generation had long dreaded a Japanese American war, and some educated Japanese Americans speculated about their future if it came. One Nisei undergraduate at Berkeley remarked in a college magazine in 1937:

What are we going to do if war does break out between United States and Japan? . . . In common language we can say "we're sunk." Even if the Nisei wanted to fight for America, what chances? Not a chance! . . . Our properties would be confiscated and most likely [we would be] herded into prison camps—perhaps we would be slaughtered on the spot.

Four months before the attack on Pearl Harbor, a Nisei businessman expressed similar fears to the Los Angeles *Times*: "We talk of almost nothing but this great crisis. We don't know what's going to happen. Sometimes we only look for a concentration camp." But Japanese Americans, too, were surprised, as often happens, when the nightmare came true.

American government agencies responsible for internal security had made contingency arrangements to intern enemy aliens if war broke out, arrangements primarily directed at the presumed threat from Nazis and Nazi sympathizers. Although such peacetime planning was regularly updated and had been accelerated when World War II broke out on September 1, 1939, it was Hitler's blitzkrieg—the lightning-like conquest of Norway, Denmark, the Low Countries, and France in April, May, and June 1940—that caused alarm in the United States. The belief that a "fifth column," internal saboteurs and subversives, had been an important factor in the fall of Western Europe led authorities in both Britain and the still neutral United States to take unprecedented measures against what proved to be a largely nonexistent threat.

In the United States the chief perceived danger came from German-born aliens, some 40,000 of whom were organized into the pro-Nazi German-American Bund. In mid-1940, as a component of a beefed-up defense program, the Roosevelt Administration's response to the threat posed by Hitler's triumphs, Congress took two steps which limited the civil rights of all noncitizens. It transferred the Immigration and Naturalization Service from the Department of Labor, essentially a protective agency, to the Department of Justice, essentially a prosecutorial agency. It also passed the Alien Registration Act, which required, for the first time in American history, that all resident aliens over fourteen years of age register annually, be fingerprinted, and report any changes of address to the government. In addition, the executive branch took a number of secret precautions. The newly established Aliens Division of the Department of Justice, in cooperation with the Federal Bureau of Investigation (FBI) and military intelligence—largely, the Office of Naval Intelligence (ONI)—drew up lists of aliens to be interned in case of war. President Roosevelt, who always liked to have multiple sources of information, set up a secret White House intelligence unit run by a journalist, John Franklin Carter. This unit, whose "agents" were mostly journalists and businessmen who collected "intelligence" on a part-time basis, was the forerunner of the Office of Strategic Services (OSS), out of which grew, in time, the Central Intelligence Agency.

Early in the fall of 1941, Carter received and relayed to the President a report on the West Coast Japanese from a businessman, Curtis B. Munson, whose "cover" was that he served a special representative of the State Department. Munson's report, while noting that the overwhelming majority of both generations were loyal and posed no threat to America, nevertheless claimed that "there are still Japanese in the United States who will tie dynamite around their waist and make a human bomb out of themselves." This was particularly dangerous, Munson reported, because the West Coast was virtually defenseless against sabotage:

> Dams, bridges, harbors, power stations, etc., are wholly unguarded. The harbor of San Pedro [Los Angeles's port] could be razed completely by four men with hand grenades and a little study in one night. Dams could be blown and half of [Southern] California could actually die of thirst . . . One railway bridge at the exit of the mountains in some cases could tie up three or four main railroads.

President Roosevelt read at least a one-page summary of Munson's report and sent it on to Secretary of War Henry L. Stimson, calling his attention to the warnings about sabotage. It is not clear that Munson's report had any direct effect. G-2, Army intelligence in Washington, drafted a reply to the President which stated that "widespread sabotage by Japanese is not expected . . . identification of dangerous Japanese on the West Coast is reasonably complete."

We now know that a major source for Munson's information was an astute naval intelligence officer, Lieutenant Commander Kenneth D. Ringle. One of a small group of naval officers who had been trained in the Japanese language, Ringle was assigned to naval headquarters in Southern California so that he could keep an eye on the Japanese community. He reported officially in 1941 "that better than 90% of the Nisei and 75% of the original immigrants were completely loyal to the United States."

Ringle could be particularly confident of his appraisal for two reasons. First, he got to know a number of Japanese Americans, some of whom willingly acted as informants about the "disloyal" minority in their community. Second, he organized, with the help of the Los Angeles police and a professional safecracker released from San Quentin prison for the task, a surreptitious break-in at the local Japanese consulate. Documents in its safe revealed that Japanese consular officials mistrusted Japanese Americans of both generations. They regarded Issei and Nisei as "cultural traitors" who could not be trusted with anything of importance. Ringle was appalled when the mass evacuation did occur and later noted with some grim satisfaction that, after "careful investigations on both the West Coast and Hawaii, there was never a shred of evidence found of sabotage, subversive acts, spying, or fifth column activity on the part of the Nisei or long-time local residents."

In the week after Pearl Harbor and the ensuing declarations of war against the United States by Germany and Italy, the Department of Justice, using the lists of presumably dangerous aliens it had prepared, rounded up and interned some three thousand enemy aliens. About half of these were Japanese. Those fifteen hundred, almost all of them males, represented a little over one percent of the nation's Japanese population. Since the government acted largely on the theory of guilt by association, it arrested most of the leaders of the Japanese community: officials of organizations, and those persons who had observable contacts with the Japanese embassy and consulates. At the same time, the Treasury Department froze the bank accounts of all enemy aliens in American banks and all the accounts in American branches of Japanese banks. It must be remembered that Japanese immigrants, unlike their German and Italian counterparts, were aliens because American law forbade their naturalization. These federal edicts paralyzed the community by depriving it of most of its leadership and its liquid assets. Later, Japanese American families were allowed to withdraw a hundred dollars a month of their own money from the blocked accounts. These official actions caused much hardship and undoubtedly, in some instances, were unjust, but they did follow due process of law and the common practice of nations. Although the later mass incarcerations are referred to as "internments," that is not really the appropriate term. In law, internment can only apply to aliens. During World War II, in the United States, internment was individual and presumably based on something the individual had done; the mass incarceration that took place was based simply on ethnic origin and geography. Each person interned had the right to an individual hearing, which, in some instances, resulted in release. There would be no such hearings for the incarcerated Japanese Americans: their "guilt" was their ancestry—although, to be sure, there were ways in which individuals could get out of the concentration camps.

All this was directed at aliens, though its effects were felt by citizens, too. But some actions were directed at citizens. On December 8, the day after Pearl Harbor, the Department of Justice issued the first federal regulation which discriminated directly against American citizens of Japanese ancestry: it closed the land borders of the United States to all enemy aliens and "all persons of Japanese ancestry, whether citizen or alien."

Left to their own devices, the internal security forces would have allowed most Japanese Americans to continue with their lives. There would have been special stress for people with a Japanese face—the face of the enemy—but most of them could have coped. But internal security was not left to the specialists: the press, the public, politicians, and some military officials began to clamor that something had to be done about the "Japs who were running around loose." This clamor was effective, in the final analysis, because, from the White House down, there was a "failure of political leadership," as the Commission on the Wartime Relocation and Internment of Civilians noted four decades later. Once anti-Japanese public and political opinion began to prevail, the internal security forces, particularly the FBI and its head, J. Edgar Hoover, joined the chorus. A contributing factor was the string of humiliating defeats that the United States and its allies suffered in the first six months of the war as Japanese imperial forces "ran wild," overrunning Hong Kong, Wake Island, the Philippines, and most of the rest of Southeast Asia, and threatening India and Australia.

In addition, the devastating defeat that Yamamoto's strike

force inflicted on the United States Navy made some of those in positions of responsibility anxious to blame someone else for their own ineptitude. The worst example of this was Secretary of the Navy Frank Knox's deliberate lying. Returning from a quick inspection of the damage at Pearl Harbor, the full scope of which was still classified, the former Chicago newspaper publisher blamed "treachery" and "the most effective fifth column work that's come out of this war, except in Norway." Knox didn't have to mention Japanese Americans by name. He knew that it was not treachery but incompetence that had allowed the Imperial Japanese Navy to strike such an effective blow. (Orders for the dismissal of Admiral Husband E. Kimmel, the naval commander in Hawaii, were already in the works.) Four days later, in a December 19 cabinet meeting at the White House, it was decided that all alien Japanese in Hawaii should be interned. This was the first post-Pearl Harbor decision about Japanese Americans to be taken at the highest levels of government, but it was never implemented.

Some of this national hysteria actually preceded Pearl Harbor. One congressman, John D. Dingell (D-Mich.), father of the present Congressman Dingell, wrote President Roosevelt on August 18, 1941, at a time when the Japanese government was making it difficult for about a hundred Americans to leave Japan, to suggest that the United States should "cause the forceful . . . imprisonment in a concentration camp of ten thousand alien Japanese in Hawaii." The Japanese attack, coming without warning and while special Japanese envoys were negotiating in Washington, set off a stream of venom, and the cry of treachery, directed at anything Japanese. On the day after Pearl Harbor the Los Angeles *Times*, the most important paper in Southern California, announced that California was "a zone of danger" and noted:

> We have thousands of Japanese here . . . Some, perhaps many . . . are good Americans. What the rest may be we do not know, nor can we take a chance in the light of yesterday's demonstration that treachery and double-dealing are major Japanese weapons.

The *Times*, which used the word "Japanese," was more polite than many West Coast papers, which habitually said "Japs" and often used terms such as "Nips," "mad dogs," and "yellow vermin." It was not just regional journalists who whipped up hysteria. Two days after Pearl Harbor, the nationally syndicated columnist Westbrook Pegler proposed that the United States adopt the methods of its enemies. For every hostage the Axis murdered, he wrote, the United States should retaliate by killing "100 victims selected out of [American] concentration camps," which Pegler assumed would be set up for subversive Germans and Italians and "alien Japanese."

Throughout the winter and into the spring, until Japanese Americans were cooped up in concentration camps, a barrage of stories stressing the presumed threat of Japanese Americans to the safety of the nation filled the press and the airwaves. The following headlines, chiefly about imaginary events, ran in the Los Angeles *Times* between December 8, 1941, and February 23, 1942:

JAP BOAT FLASHES MESSAGE ASHORE
ENEMY PLANES SIGHTED OVER CALIFORNIA COAST
TWO JAPS WITH MAPS AND ALIEN LITERATURE SEIZED
JAP AND CAMERA HELD IN BAY CITY
CAPS ON JAPANESE TOMATO PLANTS POINT TO AIR BASE
JAPANESE HERE SENT VITAL DATA TO TOKYO
CHINESE ABLE TO SPOT JAP
MAP REVEALS JAP MENACE
Network of Alien Farms Covers
Strategic Defense Areas over Southland
JAPS PLAN ATTACK IN APRIL
WARNS CHIEF OF KOREAN SPY BAND

Much of this jingoism was disseminated by the West Coast military authorities, including some who quickly regretted it. Major General Joseph W. Stilwell, not yet the famous "Vinegar Joe" of Burma fame, but already possessed of a tart tongue, was, in December 1941, the corps commander responsible for defending Southern California. He recorded in his shirt-pocket diary his day-to-day reactions, including the following:

DEC. 8—Sunday night "air raid" at San Francisco . . . Fourth Army kind of jittery.

DEC. 9—. . . Fleet of thirty-four [Japanese] ships between San Francisco and Los Angeles. Later—not authentic.

DEC. 11—[Phone call from 4th Army] "The main Japanese fleet is 164 miles off San Francisco." I believed it, like a damn fool . . . Of course [4th Army] passed the buck on this report. They had it from a "usually reliable source," but they should never have put it out without check.

DEC. 13—Not content with the above blah, [4th] Army pulled another at ten-thirty today. "Reliable information that attack on Los Angeles is imminent. A general alarm being considered . . ." What jackass would send a general alarm [which would have called for the evacuation of Los Angeles] under the circumstances. The [4th] Army G-2 [Intelligence] is just another amateur, just like all the rest of the staff. Rule: the higher the headquarters, the more important is *calm*.

The 4th Army Stilwell complained about was the San Francisco Presidio headquarters of his immediate superior, Lieutenant General John L. DeWitt, who became, on December 11, head of the newly created Western Defense Command (WDC), officially designated a Theater of Operations and made responsible for defending the entire West Coast. DeWitt, who would be put on the shelf before war's end, was a cautious, bigoted, indecisive sixty-one-year-old army bureaucrat who was a specialist in logistics. Almost twenty years earlier, as Gary Okihiro has shown, he helped prepare a plan for the militarization of Hawaii in case of war which contemplated "complete military control over . . . people, supplies, matériel . . ." and selective internment of civilians by the military. In 1941 he noted the disgrace and removal of his contemporary, Lieutenant General Walter C. Short, the army commander in Hawaii, and was determined that no such fate would befall him.

The first formal military proposal for mass incarceration went out from DeWitt's headquarters on December 19, nine days after his staff first discussed it. It recommended "that action be initiated at the earliest practicable date to collect all alien subjects fourteen years of age and over, of enemy nations and remove them" to the interior of the United States and hold them "under restraint after removal" to prevent their surreptitious return. This would have removed some 40,000 Japanese nationals, even larger numbers of Italian nationals, and smaller numbers of German nationals, many of whom were refugees from Nazism. This proposal was constitutional and generally followed statutory guidelines about internment, except that the statutes called for the internment of males only.

DeWitt's proposal soon came to the attention of Major General Allen W. Gullion in Washington, the army's Provost Marshal General (PMG), in effect its top cop. Gullion, one-time Judge Advocate General, the army's highest legal-affairs officer, had since the fall of France in mid-1940 been studying how the army could exercise control over civilians. At that time, military intelligence, acting on the false premise that fifth-column activity had been a major factor in the German victories, made the assumption that, in case of war, the U.S. military forces would "through their Provost Marshal Generals . . . certainly have to provide for the arrest and holding of a large number of suspects," alien and citizen. This would have expanded greatly the numbers of troops reporting to the PMG and made him a likely candidate for promotion. Unfortunately for Gullion's ambitions, the President had given the Justice Department, not the War Department, the responsibility for countering subversive activities and control over civilian enemy aliens.

On December 22 Gullion formally requested Secretary of War Stimson to try to get the enemy-alien program transferred from civilian to military control. When Stimson's office showed no interest—the Secretary of War and his Chief of Staff, George C. Marshall, wanted all military energies focused on getting American armies ready for combat—Gullion went outside channels and telephoned General DeWitt in San Francisco directly.* Gullion told the West Coast commander that a representative of the Los Angeles Chamber of Commerce had come to see him and urged that all Japanese there should be locked up.

* Happily for historians, the army regularly recorded many of its phone calls on wax cylinders and often transcribed them for circulation. This was not surreptitious wire-tapping; both army parties knew that the calls were being recorded. Outsiders who called in may not have been aware of the system.

Gullion tried to get DeWitt to recommend a roundup of citizen Japanese as well as the aliens he had suggested a week earlier. On December 26 the WDC commander told Gullion that he was opposed to rounding up citizens.

> I'm very doubtful that it would be common sense procedure to try and intern 117,000 Japanese in this theater . . . An American citizen, after all, is an American citizen. And while they may not be loyal, I think we can weed the disloyal out of the loyal and lock them up if necessary.

DeWitt told Gullion that he opposed military control of alien civilians: "It would be better if this thing worked through the civil channels." Unfortunately, DeWitt did not adhere to those "common sense" views. It is impossible to know what, exactly, changed his mind, but a reading of hundreds of pages of transcripts of his telephone conversations shows that he was inconsistent about many things and was susceptible to the influence of the last strong personality he had talked to.

If Gullion had little effect on DeWitt, he and his subordinates did manage to get the Department of Justice to make further inroads into the constitutional rights of Japanese Americans. On December 30 Attorney General Francis Biddle informed Gullion's office that, as the PMG had requested, he had authorized warrantless raids on Japanese American homes in which at least one of the residents was an enemy alien. In other words, if a Nisei family had an Issei grandmother living with it, the Fourth Amendment constitutional protection against "unreasonable searches and seizures" no longer applied. A literal reign of terror was conducted in Japanese American communities in the following weeks; hundreds and perhaps thousands of individual homes were searched. A teenage Nisei girl from San Jose told of coming home

> to find two F.B.I. men at our front door. They asked permission to search the house. One man looked through the front rooms, while the other searched the back rooms. Trembling with fright, I followed and watched each of the men look around. The investigators examined the mat-

tresses, and the dressers and looked under the beds. The gas range, piano and sofa were thoroughly inspected. Since I was the only one at home, the F.B.I. questioned me, but did not produce sufficient evidence of Fifth Columnists in our family. This made me very happy, even if they did mess up the house.

From late December until the decision to evacuate all Japanese Americans from the West Coast was made in mid-February, the Provost Marshal and his subordinates put extraordinary pressure on the civilian officials of the Justice Department. The military bureaucrats always insisted that what they wanted was dictated by military necessity, and the Attorney General's men reluctantly but steadily beat a retreat. More and more constitutional protections were stripped from Japanese Americans. According to Gullion, the Justice Department's representatives, James Rowe, Jr., an Assistant Attorney General and former special assistant to President Roosevelt, and Edward J. Ennis, head of the Aliens Division, were constantly apologizing about the slowness of their department, while Gullion complained steadily that Attorney General Biddle was "not functioning" and threatened to have Secretary Stimson protest to the President that the civilians in the Justice Department were holding up the war effort.

The competing Washington groups each sent emissaries to DeWitt's San Francisco headquarters: Rowe for the Justice Department, and Major Karl R. Bendetsen, Ennis's military counterpart, as chief of the Aliens Division of the PMG's office. Bendetsen, a 1932 graduate of Stanford Law School, had gone on active duty as a captain in 1940 and while supervising the rounding up and incarceration of the Japanese Americans would win a colonel's eagles before he was thirty-five. His arrival at the Presidio set up a regular though unauthorized channel of communication between DeWitt's headquarters and the PMG's office. This bypassing of Chief of Staff George C. Marshall and his immediate subordinates meant that they had little input into or even knowledge of what the army's official history later called "the plans and decisions for Japanese evacuation."

Bendetsen produced a plan which DeWitt adopted and to

which the Justice Department reluctantly agreed. All enemy aliens were to be reregistered, photographed, and fingerprinted: the resulting documents were to be kept in duplicate; one set where the alien lived, another in a central office. This bureaucratic record-keeping was to enable the army to set up a "pass and permit" system, dividing the West Coast into Category A and Category B zones. The former were for key installations; the latter, for the rest of the coastal region. As late as February 3, Assistant Secretary of War John J. McCloy spoke of this program as the "best way to solve" the West Coast Japanese problem. He envisaged establishing

> limited restricted areas around the airplane plants, the forts and other important military installations . . . We might call these military reservations in substance and exclude everyone—whites, yellows, blacks, greens—from the area and then license back into the area those whom we felt there was no danger to be expected from . . . Then we can cover the legal situation . . . in spite of the constitution . . . You may, by that process, eliminate all the Japs [alien and citizen] but you might conceivably permit some to come back whom you are quite certain are free from any suspicion.

McCloy had gone to the heart of the situation: how to do what the army wanted to do, "in spite of the constitution." Although the oath of office that he and others took pledged them to "preserve and protect" the Constitution, they spent untold hours trying, with eventual success, to get around the fact that, under the Constitution, the vast majority of Japanese Americans were citizens with the same rights and obligations as any other citizens.

The army, and eventually the Selective Service System, which administered the military draft, clearly violated the law in their treatment of the Japanese. Before Pearl Harbor, Japanese Americans had been treated like other citizens and, by November 1941, more than three thousand had been inducted into the armed forces. Others had enlisted or entered service with National Guard units. The 1940 peacetime draft law was one of the first federal statutes to contain a clear non-discrimination clause:

> In classifying a registrant there shall be no discrimination for or against him because of his race, creed or color, because of his membership or activity in any labor, political, religious or other organization. Each registrant shall receive equal and fair justice.

Non-discrimination, however, did not apply once a draftee entered the military; blacks were universally segregated and political radicals were often mistreated and barred from promotion. After Pearl Harbor, many, but not all, military commands began discharging Japanese Americans, and many local draft boards stopped drafting them, usually classifying them 4-F—physically or mentally unfit for service. Eventually, the Selective Service System sent out an illegal directive to all draft boards instructing them to classify all men of Japanese ancestry, regardless of citizenship, as 4-C, a category previously reserved for enemy aliens.

Selective Service and other federal offices which violated laws in their treatment of Japanese Americans had no need to be concerned about being called to account by Congress. Many members of Congress urged the government to "do something" about the West Coast Japanese, and complained throughout the war that the government was "coddling Japs." In mid-December, for example, John Rankin (D-Miss.) called for "deporting every Jap." A month later, Leland Ford (R-Calif.) urged War Secretary Stimson to have "all Japanese, whether citizen or not . . . placed in inland concentration camps." Although letters from members of Congress usually get rapid responses, Stimson and his staff thought for ten days about how to answer Ford's letter. Then, in a letter drafted by Bendetsen, Stimson agreed with the congressman and took the opportunity to disparage his cabinet colleague Francis Biddle. Although "the internment of over a hundred thousand people involves many complex considerations," the war secretary wrote, "the Army is prepared to provide internment facilities." He noted, however, that it was Biddle's responsibility, that the army had to submit suggestions to him, and closed by encouraging Ford to present his views to the Attorney General.

Not all federal officials were anxious to violate the rights of

Japanese Americans. In addition to the reluctant lawyers in the Justice Department, many New Dealers were appalled by what was happening to the West Coast Japanese. A group of Department of Agriculture field staff, for example, reported to Secretary of Agriculture Claude Wickard in early January that sporadic violence against rural Japanese had left much of that population "terrified."

> They do not leave their homes at night . . . The police authorities are probably not sympathetic to the Japanese and are giving them only the minimum protection. Investigation of actual attacks on Japanese have been merely perfunctory and no prosecutions have been initiated.

Wickard's staff, whose wartime assignment was to maximize agricultural production, advised the Secretary to take positive steps to protect the property and the person of Japanese farmers and thus maintain production. Wickard waffled. He urged Stimson not to allow California's production of vegetables to be curtailed, suggested removing Japanese Americans from the coastal areas and putting them in the central valleys of California, where they could continue to produce crops, and pointed out that Mexicans could be imported to do the work that Japanese could no longer do.

Late in January, Chief of Staff George C. Marshall asked the PMG's office to prepare a memorandum on the "Japanese American problem." This is the first evidence we have that he was aware of it. On January 24, Bendetsen phoned DeWitt to ask what he would suggest if "the Department of Justice still fails to do what we think they ought to do." DeWitt, who hoped that Justice would come around, spoke of his anxieties about sabotage: "We know that [Japanese Americans] are communicating [with the Japanese Navy] at sea." This was not true, but DeWitt undoubtedly believed it. Then, in a logic-defying leap, DeWitt insisted that "the fact that we have [not even] sporadic attempts at sabotage clearly means that control is being exercised somewhere." Here was the "heads I win, tails you lose" proposition that Joseph Heller would later call "Catch 22" in his novel about World War II. If there had been sabotage, DeWitt would have had an excuse to remove Japanese Americans from his command. Since there wasn't, there must be a conspiracy not to commit sabotage until America dropped its guard. Therefore, the "logic" ran, evacuate the potential saboteurs before they could do any damage. As foolish as this argument sounds, it convinced many Americans.

The Attorney General of California, Earl Warren, for example, after meeting with DeWitt, told a congressional committee in February:

> Unfortunately [many] are of the opinion that because we have had no sabotage and no fifth column activities in this State . . . that means that none have been planned for us. But . . . this is the most ominous sign in our whole situation . . . The fifth column activities that we are to get, are timed, just like the invasion of France, and of Norway . . . I believe that we are just being lulled into a false sense of security . . . Our day of reckoning is bound to come.

Warren, later a great Chief Justice of the Supreme Court, would regret these and other anti-Japanese words and deeds until his dying day and apologized for them in his memoirs.

One reason that the fifth-column metaphor was so effective was that it came from high authority. As we have seen, Navy Secretary Knox used it in a December press conference; in late January, it was used in a public report, this time by an Associate Justice of the Supreme Court, Owen J. Roberts. Sent to Hawaii by President Roosevelt to head a committee of inquiry into the disaster at Pearl Harbor, Roberts concluded, correctly, that the unpreparedness of Hawaii's military commanders had been a major factor in the disaster. But, in addition, Roberts reported —falsely—that a Japanese American fifth column had aided the attackers. His report also criticized the laxity of American counter-espionage activity in the islands and implied that the FBI had been inhibited because it paid too much attention to the Constitution! Such criticism from a Supreme Court Justice spurred the growing demand for removal of the Japanese Americans. Roberts also told Secretary Stimson privately that his panel felt that "dangerous Japanese in Hawaii" were a special

threat, a warning that could only have heightened the fears of
the war secretary about the safety of key West Coast aircraft
plants such as the Boeing plant outside Seattle, the North
American and Lockheed plants in Los Angeles, and the Vultee
plant in San Diego.

The press and radio played up these official announcements
and spread false and foolish rumors. The most popular was the
report that American university class rings had been found on
the fingers of the few Japanese fliers shot down during the raid
on Pearl Harbor. In Southern California papers, they were
UCLA or USC rings; in northern California, they were from
Stanford or the University of California at Berkeley; and in the
Pacific Northwest, they were from schools in that area. These
canards were not spread just by gutter journalists. Edward R.
Murrow, as close to a patron saint as American journalism has
produced, told a Seattle audience at the end of January:

> I think it's probable that, if Seattle ever does get bombed,
> you will be able to look up and see some University of
> Washington sweaters on the boys doing the bombing!

By the end of January, in preparation for a meeting with the
House delegations from the Pacific Coast, Bendetsen coordinated some new proposals with DeWitt. The transcript of the
telephone conversation reads:

BENDETSEN: . . . Summarizing our conversation, you are of the
opinion that there will have to be an evacuation on the
West Coast, not only of Japanese aliens but also of Japanese
citizens, that is you would include citizens along with alien
enemies, and that if you had the power of requisition over
all other federal agencies, if you were requested you would
be willing on the coast to accept responsibility for the alien
enemy program.

DEWITT: Yes I would. And I think its got to come sooner or
later.

BENDETSEN: Yes sir, I do too, and I think the subject may be
discussed tomorrow at the congressional delegation meeting.

Bendetsen's meeting with the House delegations took place on January 30. Rowe and Ennis from the Justice Department also attended. Although Bendetsen reported officially that he was just "an observer," his post-meeting telephone call to General DeWitt reveals him as an advocate of the policies he and General Gullion wanted to put into effect.

BENDETSEN: They asked me to state what the position of the War Department was. I stated that I could not speak for the War Department . . . They asked me for my own views and I stated that the position of the War Department was this: that we did not seek control of the program, that we preferred it be handled by the civil agencies. However, the War Department would be entirely willing, I believed, [to assume] the responsibility provided they accorded the War Department, and the Secretary of War, and the military commander under him, full authority to require the services of any federal agency, and required that federal agency was required to respond.

This last provision—military supremacy over civilian agencies —particularly pleased DeWitt, who was annoyed with FBI officials, such as the San Francisco agent-in-charge, who had pooh-poohed some of DeWitt's fears about the Japanese. As the general put it:

DEWITT: Mr. [J. Edgar] Hoover himself as head of the F.B.I. would have to function under the War Department exactly as he is functioning under the Department of Justice.

Bendetsen called DeWitt the next day, February 1, to make sure that the often vacillating general had not changed his mind. When asked whether he intended to move citizens, the Western Defense Command chief was emphatic:

DEWITT: I include all Germans, all Italians who are alien enemies and all Japanese who are native-born or foreign born . . . evacuate enemy aliens in large groups at the earliest possible date . . . sentiment is being given too much importance

. . . handle these people as they should be handled . . . I
place the following priority . . . First the Japanese . . . the
most dangerous . . . the next group, the Germans . . . the
third group, the Italians . . . We've waited too long as it is.
Get them all out.

The same day, February 1, McCloy, Gullion, and Bendetsen
went to Attorney General Biddle's office to try to coordinate the
policies of the two arms of the executive branch. Biddle and his
associates had drafted a press release that they hoped the War
Department would agree to issue jointly—evidence of how little
they comprehended what the military was planning. Its crucial
sentences read:

The Department of War and the Department of Justice are
in agreement that the present military situation does not at
this time require the removal of American citizens of the
Japanese race. The Secretary of War, General DeWitt, the
Attorney General, and the Director of the Federal Bureau
of Investigation believe that appropriate steps have been
and are being taken.

The men from the War Department refused to agree. According to General Gullion's account of the meeting, Attorney
General Biddle stated that he was opposed to mass evacuation
and that the Justice Department would have nothing to do with
it. Gullion, admittedly "a little sore," demanded of the Attorney
General: "Do you mean to tell me that if the Army, the men on
the ground, determine it is a military necessity to move citizens,
Jap citizens, that you won't help us?" After Biddle again said
that he would not, Assistant Secretary of War McCloy re-
sponded: "You are putting a Wall Street lawyer in a helluva
box, but if it is a question of the safety of the country [and] the
Constitution . . . Why the Constitution is just a scrap of paper
to me."

Although the Philadelphia patrician Francis Biddle, F.D.R.'s
fourth Attorney General, was a civil libertarian—as befitted a
former law clerk of Justice Oliver Wendell Holmes—when war
came, he proved incapable of resisting the demands of the

military. He could stand up to McCloy, but, as he admits ruefully in his memoirs, he was overawed by the other patrician in the cabinet, Secretary of War Stimson, who had been Secretary of War in President Taft's cabinet when Biddle was a schoolboy.

On February 2, the day after the conference in Biddle's office, powerful legislative forces began to move. A senior Republican, California's Senator Hiram W. Johnson, coordinated the activities of the entire West Coast congressional delegation, which met that day and the next to decide what to recommend about their Japanese American constituents. Johnson, who had masterminded a similar group in the 1924 fight for Japanese exclusion, was more concerned with defense against an invasion by Japanese military forces than he was about sabotage and complained that interest in the "Japanese question . . . far overshadowed" interest in preparedness. Although the delegation would make no recommendation until February 13, Washington insiders knew what was afoot.

On February 3, two days after the conference in Biddle's office, McCloy and General Marshall made separate telephone calls to DeWitt, apparently because each was concerned that subordinate officers—DeWitt and Gullion—were committing the War Department to a policy that had not yet been agreed to. The Assistant Secretary of War was blunt:

MCCLOY: . . . the Army, that means you in the area, should not take the position, even in your conversations with political figures out there [favoring] a wholesale withdrawal of Japanese citizens and aliens from the Coast . . . We have about reached the point where we feel that perhaps the best solution of it is to limit the withdrawal to certain prohibited areas.

DEWITT: Mr. Secretary . . . I haven't taken any position.

DeWitt was simply lying, as transcripts of telephone conversations and other documents demonstrate. However, DeWitt had not yet made any such recommendations in writing, and, clearly, McCloy did not yet have copies of the telephone transcripts.

That same day Stimson, McCloy, Gullion, and Bendetsen met for an hour and a half. The next day Gullion reported that

Stimson and McCloy "are against any mass movement. They are pretty much against it. And they are also pretty much against interfering with civilians unless it can be done legally."

Two days later, on February 5, DeWitt himself seemed to be backing away from mass evacuation. After conferring with James Rowe of the Justice Department and Governor Culbert Olson of California, the WDC commander seemed willing "merely" to have Japanese Americans moved from the coastal zone to the interior of California. There, according to DeWitt, the governor wanted to put them to work on arable and tillable land.

> They are going to keep them in the state. They don't want to bring in a lot of negroes and mexicans and let them take their place . . . They just want to put them on the land out of the cities where they can raise vegetables like they are doing now.

These developments disgusted the PMG's men, who had visions of their plans being frustrated. Colonel Archer Lerch, Gullion's deputy, complained on the telephone to Bendetsen:

> I think I detect a decided weakening on the part of Gen. DeWitt, which I think is most unfortunate . . . The idea . . . that a satisfactory solution must be reached through a conference between the Governor and leading Jap-Americans, savors too much of the spirit of Rotary and overlooks the necessary cold-bloodedness of war.

But just at this time—the first days of February 1942— political pressures from the West Coast increased in number and intensity, in part because of false information disseminated by the military. The erratic Governor Olson in a much-publicized radio report to the already frightened people of California on February 4 maintained:

> It is known that there are Japanese residents of California who have sought to aid the Japanese enemy by way of communicating information, or have shown indications of preparation for fifth column activities.

During the next two days the mayor of Los Angeles, Fletcher Bowron, rang changes on the same theme:

> Right here in our own city are those who may spring to action at an appointed time in accordance with a prearranged plan wherein each of our little Japanese friends will know his part in the event of any possible attempted invasion or air raid . . . We cannot run the risk of another Pearl Harbor episode in Southern California.

Back in Washington, the PMG and his associates continued to press their civilian chiefs. On February 5 and 6 Gullion marshaled his arguments for mass movement and presented them to McCloy. He repeated the false statement that there were "reliable reports from military and other sources [that] the danger of Japanese inspired sabotage is great" and warned McCloy, with some of the journalistic buzz words of the time, that measures short of mass evacuation would be "too little or too late." Gullion had no detailed plans, but his basic proposal called for interning all Japanese aliens, accompanied by citizen members of their families, in camps east of the Sierra Nevada mountains. Since about half the Nisei were still minors, this would involve the majority of the Japanese American population. By February 10 McCloy had apparently been convinced that mass evacuation was necessary, but Secretary Stimson still adhered to the notion that creating what some officials referred to as "Jap-free islands" around strategic defense establishments was all that was really appropriate. By the next day, February 11, the war secretary had changed his mind. Sometime that afternoon he telephoned Franklin Roosevelt in the White House to recommend mass evacuation. Since Stimson did not allow the President's calls to be recorded, we do not know exactly what was said, but later that afternoon McCloy telephoned Bendetsen in San Francisco with the good news.

MCCLOY: . . . we talked to the President and the President, in substance, says go ahead and do anything you think necessary . . . if it involves citizens, we will take care of them too. He says that there will probably be some repercussions, but it has got to be dictated by military necessity, but as he puts it, 'Be as reasonable as you can.' [McCloy's "we" should not be taken literally. Stimson alone talked to F.D.R.]

At about the time that the civilians who ran the army made their decision, the military planners were reaching an opposite conclusion. Chief of Staff Marshall had assigned Brigadier General Mark W. Clark to evaluate the threat posed by the West Coast Japanese, and he quickly became the general-headquarters staff "expert" on the topic, although as late as February 4 Clark had to ask Bendetsen, "Now, what is this Nisei?" Based simply on military expediency, Clark disagreed with the recommendation for a "mass exodus" and maintained that there was no perfect defense against sabotage and that the use of undue military means and energy could sabotage "our entire offensive effort." Using Gullion's empire-building figures, Clark estimated that it would take 10,000 to 15,000 soldiers to guard interned Japanese, even if only aliens were incarcerated. Clark proposed, instead, selecting critical installations—he named the Boeing plant and the Bremerton Navy Yard in Washington—and ejecting all enemy aliens from their vicinity, and permitting the entry of all others by pass only. Civilian police and the FBI would be the responsible security forces.

General Clark was not a civil libertarian. He recommended making frequent raids—"ring leaders and suspects should be interned liberally"—and a campaign of terror by propaganda:

This alien group should be made to understand through publicity that the first overt act on their part will bring a wave of counter-measures which will make the historical efforts of the vigilantes look puny in comparison.

But General Clark's proposal, which would have incarcerated no one, embodied the real "military necessity." It came late, however, a day after the conservative Republican political leaders of the War Department had gotten the President's nod for a policy of mass evacuation. A few liberals, such as Archibald MacLeish, director of the Office of Facts and Figures, the predecessor of the Office of War Information, tried to emphasize the importance of maintaining civil liberty, but to no avail. Of more significance was the column by Walter Lippmann published on February 12, the day of Clark's report. Lippmann, the most influential American columnist, was writing from San Francisco, where he had interviewed General DeWitt. In an essay titled "The Fifth Column on the Coast," the journalist stated:

> . . . the Pacific Coast is in imminent danger of a combined attack from within and without . . . It is a fact that the Japanese navy has been reconnoitering the coast more or less continuously* . . . There is an assumption [in Washington] that a citizen may not be interfered with unless he has committed an overt act . . . The Pacific Coast is a combat zone: Some part of it may at any moment be a battlefield. And nobody ought to be on a battlefield who has no good reason for being there. There is plenty of room elsewhere for him to exercise his rights.

The next day, February 13, the Pacific Coast congressional delegation sent President Roosevelt a unanimous recommendation urging

> the immediate evacuation of all persons of Japanese lineage and all others, aliens and citizens alike, whose presence shall be deemed dangerous or inimical to the defense of the United States from [eventually] the states of California, Oregon and Washington, and the Territory of Alaska.

Four days later, on February 17, Attorney General Biddle, the only cabinet officer on record as actively opposing mass evacuation, sent a memorandum to the President which strongly attacked West Coast pressure groups and congressmen who were urging evacuation and blasted Lippmann and other columnists who were acting as "Armchair Strategists and Junior

---

* This was undoubtedly what DeWitt told him, but it was not true. German naval vessels in the Atlantic were closer to San Francisco in February 1942 than any surface vessels of the Imperial Japanese Navy.

G-Men," but it said nothing about his cabinet colleague Stimson or his associates. Then, in a curious sentence which seemed to accept the notion of mass evacuation, he warned that "so large a job must be done after careful planning."

On February 19, 1942, a "day of infamy" as far as the Constitution is concerned, Franklin Roosevelt signed Executive Order 9066,* which was the instrument by which just over 120,000 persons, two-thirds of them American citizens, were confined in concentration camps on American soil, in some cases for nearly four years. Yet the document itself is strangely reticent. It mentions no ethnic or racial group by name, nor does it specify place. President Roosevelt delegated to the Secretary of War and to "the Military Commanders whom he may . . . designate" the authority to name "military areas" from which "any or all persons may be excluded" and indicated that "transportation, food, shelter, and other accommodations" may be provided for such persons "until other arrangements are made." All this was in the name of the "successful prosecution of the war," which lawyers later shortened to "military necessity."

This elliptical legal language was not intended to fool anyone. The press was given guidance by military and civilian public-relations officers, so that the American public was immediately informed that the Japanese, because they posed a threat to national security, were going to be removed from California and put somewhere else under guard. A few, including the President himself, publicly used the words "concentration camp" to describe the places where the Japanese were sent. Later, after the discovery of the Nazi death camps, many shied away from using the term "concentration camp" to describe the sites where the American government confined 120,000 persons who were guilty of nothing other than being ethnically Japanese. The American camps were not death camps, but they were surrounded by barbed wire and by troops whose guns were pointed at the inmates. Almost all the 1,862 Japanese Americans who died in them died of natural causes, and they were outnumbered by the 5,918 American citizens who were born in the concentration camps. But the few Japanese Americans who were killed

---

* See Document 1 for text of Executive Order 9066.

"accidentally" by their American guards were just as dead as the millions of Jews and others who were killed deliberately by their German, Soviet, or Japanese guards.

The reasons for the establishment of these concentration camps are clear. A deteriorating military situation created the opportunity for American racists to get their views accepted by the national leadership. The Constitution was treated as a scrap of paper not only by McCloy, Stimson, and Roosevelt but also by the entire Congress, which approved and implemented everything done to the Japanese Americans, and by the Supreme Court of the United States, which in December 1944, nearly three years after the fact, in effect sanctioned the incarceration of the Japanese Americans.

The Court has always held that the "war power" and the right of national defense could stretch the limits of federal authority, and Roosevelt and the lawyers in the War Department who drafted Executive Order 9066 appealed to that power. But was there a "military necessity" for EO 9066? As noted, the general staff officer charged with assessing the West Coast situation did not think so, and the army's G-2 (intelligence) reported to General Marshall, on the very day Roosevelt signed the order, that its analysts believed that "mass evacuation [was] unnecessary." The decision made was not military but political: the general staff was not asked for its opinion, and its official recommendations were ignored. When the cases testing the constitutionality of the actions taken against the Japanese Americans came before the Supreme Court in 1943 and 1944, the War and Justice Departments not only suppressed this evidence but also, as Peter Irons has demonstrated, deliberately presented false reports of subversion to the Court.

Perhaps the best way to appreciate the difference between real and fictitious military necessity is to contrast the way in which the federal government treated the Japanese on the West Coast and the Japanese in Hawaii. On the West Coast, despite continuing panic of the kind described by General Stilwell in December, there had been only desultory and largely harmless shellings by two Japanese submarines. Hawaii had been severely bombed and seemed vulnerable to further attack. In California, Japanese of all generations constituted some 2 percent of the population, whereas in Hawaii every third person was of Japanese ethnicity. Yet in Hawaii there was only minimal incarceration of Japanese: out of a population of some 150,000, fewer than 1,500 persons were confined. And when, throughout the first few months of the war, politicians—most persistently, Secretary of the Navy Knox—called for mass incarceration in Hawaii, the nation's highest military commanders successfully resisted the pressure, not because of any concern for the civil rights of the Hawaiian Japanese, but because Japanese labor was crucial to both the civilian and the military economies in Hawaii.

Although others worked out the details and made the plans, it was Franklin D. Roosevelt, America's greatest modern President, who signed Executive Order 9066 and must bear whatever blame history records. Merely signing the vague executive order in February 1942, however, did not spell out the fate of the Japanese Americans.

3

LIFE BEHIND

BARBED WIRE, 1942–1946

WHILE politicians and generals decided their fate, the Japanese American people could only wait in nervous anticipation. Until March 2, 1942, nearly three months after Pearl Harbor, the constitutional rights of those Japanese who were American citizens were not generally abridged, except that they were not allowed to leave the country. But the Issei generation were not and could not become American citizens and thus were "enemy aliens." Their bank accounts and other liquid assets were frozen, which naturally affected their citizen children. It was possible for Japanese American families to leave the West Coast, although relatively few had either the assets or the will to do so; for most of them, the rest of the United States was terra incognita, and few wished to face unknown dangers in unfamiliar territory. Several thousand did pack up and try to relocate in other states, but most quickly returned when they encountered frightening hostility. An official government report described it this way:

> [Japanese Americans] who tried to cross into the interior states ran into all kinds of trouble. Some were turned back by armed posses at the border of Nevada; others were clapped into jail and held overnight by panicky local peace officers; nearly all had difficulty in buying gasoline; many were greeted by "No Japs Wanted" signs on the main streets of interior communities; and a few were threatened, or felt that they were threatened, with possibilities of mob violence.

As these refugees returned to the West Coast, their stories must have discouraged others from even trying to leave. On February 14, in a move not coordinated with any other government action, the United States Navy posted notices on Terminal Island, part of the port of Los Angeles and home to some five hundred families of Japanese fishermen, telling all the Japanese that they would have to leave by March 14. But on February 25 new signs went up, saying that they all had to leave by midnight of February 27. The navy didn't care where the fishermen and their families went; most moved elsewhere in the L.A. area and were later moved again by the army. The army could have used a similar procedure and simply evicted those Japanese who lived adjacent to military or other strategic facilities, as Secretary Stimson had wanted to do. That option was not taken, and for a time it was not certain what was going to be done with the Japanese American people, though the public on the West Coast had been assured that something would be done.

At the end of February, a select committee of the House of Representatives which had been set up in 1940 to investigate "national defense migration" held hearings in four West Coast cities about the situation of the Japanese Americans. Like the general public, the congressmen were not clear what was going to be done. Officials of the Japanese American Citizens League, the only Japanese American organization which arranged to testify, made it known that they would cooperate: national secretary Mike Masaoka testified to the organization's "complete agreement" with "any policy of evacuation definitely arising from reasons of military necessity." National treasurer Hito Okada went even further, telling the lawmakers that he believed "that the aliens should be evacuated," and in response to a direct question from the chair, Representative John Tolan (D-Calif.) said that, while he hadn't made up his mind about that, "if it [was] necessary, from the danger standpoint, then all should be evacuated." And so it went, up and down the Coast. Of the fifteen Japanese Americans who appeared, only two, James and Caryl Omura, a brother and sister who published a tiny Nisei magazine (circulation ca. 500) as an avocation, opposed mass evacuation as a violation of the rights of citizens of Japanese ancestry.

The congressmen obviously viewed the impending removal of at least some of the West Coast Japanese with equanimity and in some cases with relief. And Chairman Tolan had signed the February 13 congressional recommendation for evacuation "of all persons of Japanese lineage." But proposals to move Italian American aliens—no one even contemplated moving Caucasian citizens—were viewed unsympathetically. Tolan encouraged an Italian American attorney to "tell us about the DiMaggios," and the committee heard that although the parents of Joe DiMaggio, who had just set a still-standing major-league baseball record by getting a base hit in fifty-six straight games, were "not citizens" despite decades of residence in the United States, it would not be good policy to force such honest, law-abiding persons to move. The same arguments could have been made for the vast majority of the American Japanese, except, of course, that none were parents of a famous star. Alien Italian Americans and alien German Americans did not escape totally unscathed. Many were forced to move out of supposedly sensitive areas, and even the elder DiMaggio was unable to continue fishing from San Francisco's Fisherman's Wharf. Thousands of German and Italian aliens whose names appeared on the government's lists were interned, and in many instances, citizen wives and minor children accompanied them. But no white citizens of German or Italian birth or ancestry were deprived of their liberty by the government except by individual warrant and according to due process of law. (This is not to say that those interned were dangerous or that no injustices were committed in their internment.)

Only on March 2 did DeWitt's disorganized headquarters begin the process of restriction, removal, and incarceration which Executive Order 9066 had authorized. On that day the West Coast commander issued Public Proclamation No. 1, which divided the states of Washington, Oregon, California, and Arizona into two "Military Areas"—No. 1 and No. 2. No. 1 was further subdivided into a "prohibited zone," which ran along the Pacific shore, and a "restricted zone" (see Map 1). In addition,

MAP 1
West Coast Military Zones, 1942–1945

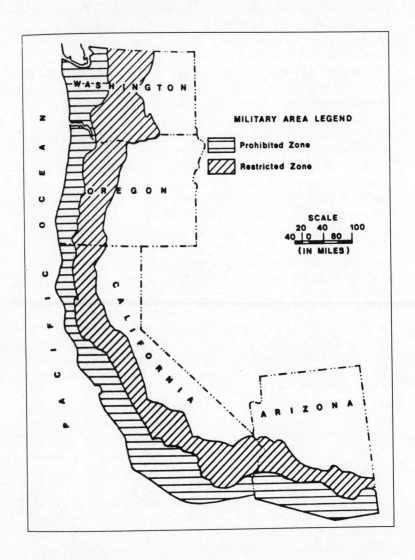

Source: Adapted from U.S. Department of War, *Final Report: Japanese Evacuation from the West Coast 1942* (Washington, D.C., 1943), Fig. 8, p. 87

ninety-eight small zones around presumably strategic places or installations were also designated "prohibited."

The proclamation did not force anyone to move; nor did it explain what procedures would be followed; DeWitt and his subordinates had not worked that out yet. But it did name its targets: "Japanese, German or Italian" aliens and "any person of Japanese ancestry." An accompanying press release suggested that all Japanese would be excluded from "Area No. 1" and the "prohibited areas" and explicitly stated—falsely, as it turned out—that no "prohibition, regulation or restriction" was contemplated for "Area No. 2."

Two weeks later DeWitt issued a second proclamation, establishing four more military areas—numbered 3 to 6—covering the entire states of Idaho, Montana, Nevada, and Utah, and 933 more small prohibited zones. We now know that DeWitt planned to round up the Japanese in those states, too, "so there won't be any Japanese in the Western Defense Command," but the War Department wouldn't let him. Japanese Americans who lived in those states or had moved there from the West Coast remained at liberty.

Proclamation No. 3, effective March 27, was the first which directly violated the rights of most Japanese Americans, including citizens, and regulated their daily lives: it instituted, throughout both parts of Military Area No. 1, an 8 p.m. to 6 a.m. curfew for "all enemy aliens" and "persons of Japanese ancestry." During the day they were restricted to "their place of . . . employment" or "not more than five miles from their place of residence." They could continue to move out of the Military Area, but that last escape hatch was closed by March 30, when all Japanese persons—but not Caucasian enemy aliens—were forbidden to leave Military Area No. 1. Thus, the vast majority of Japanese Americans were in a trap by the end of March 1942. How and when it would snap shut was not yet clear, but few now doubted that snap it would.

Congress had already provided the means to close the jaws of DeWitt's trap by enacting, at the army's request, Public Law No. 503, which made it a federal crime for anyone ordered to leave a "military area" to refuse to do so. This extraordinary law, which could have been applied to anyone, meant that, though martial law had not been declared, a general in the continental United States could, at will, order about any citizen in a Military Area. Senator Robert A. Taft (R-Ohio) declared on the floor of the Senate that it was the "sloppiest" criminal law he had ever seen, but since he had been assured that it would be used only against the Japanese, he would vote for it. It passed both houses without a single dissenting vote.

Just three days later, on March 24, 1942, DeWitt issued Civilian Exclusion Order No. 1, which was a dress rehearsal for the movement of all the West Coast Japanese from limited freedom to incarceration. It affected only some fifty Japanese families living on Bainbridge Island in Puget Sound, a short ferry ride from Seattle. They were sent, by train, all the way to Manzanar, in Southern California, because the army did not have a facility in the Pacific Northwest ready to receive them. After getting rid of the Bainbridge Islanders, the army, with the aid of technocrats on loan from the Census Bureau, divided the rest of the West Coast into 107 evacuation districts, each with approximately a thousand Japanese in them. No overall announcement was made about who would go when: the army's cat-and-mouse game called for secrecy so that advance notice "would not reach any affected person within the evacuation district." Eventually, both parts of Military Area No. 1 and the California parts of Military Area No. 2 were evacuated, but the Japanese living in eastern Washington and Oregon and most of Arizona did not have to move. (See Map 1.) The evacuation districts were methodically emptied of Japanese. By early June 1942, every Japanese person in the affected area was supposed to be in custody. (We now know that one Japanese, the Nisei Fred T. Korematsu, went underground and avoided custody for a few weeks. There may have been others who were not caught.)

The Army established a standard timetable for evacuation.
A. Posting of the Exclusion Order (a separate one was issued for each district establishing its boundaries) throughout the area: From 12:00 noon of the first day to 5:00 A.M. the second day.
B. Registration of all persons of Japanese ancestry within the

area: From 8:00 A.M. to 5:00 P.M. on the second and third days.

C. Processing, or preparing evacuees for evacuation: from 8:00 A.M. to 5:00 P.M. the fourth and fifth days.

D. Movement of evacuees in increments of approximately 500: On the sixth and seventh days.

The notices, placed on telephone poles and in store windows, told people where and when to report and that they could bring with them only what they could carry. They were ordered to supply their own "bedding and linen (no mattress)," "toilet articles," "extra clothing," "knives, forks, spoons, plates, bowls and cups," and "essential personal effects." No pets were allowed, so in Japanese communities family pets were given away or, in many cases, destroyed. The army did not allow the shipment of household goods to camp, so people had to sell, give away, or discard what they could not carry. Those with cars and trucks were not allowed to drive themselves to camp—in fact, the army kept the destinations secret—so vehicles had to be disposed of, too. Most goods were sold at "bargain" prices: the buyers knew that the owners had to sell. One woman remembered, years later, that her mother smashed her wedding dishes, brought from Japan, one by one rather than sell them for a pittance.

Unlike the Bainbridge Islanders, most Japanese went to one of fifteen improvised camps fairly close to their homes. Most people boarded trains or were loaded onto trucks or buses, and taken to the nearest camp. These assembly centers, as they were called, stretched from Puyallup, Washington, to Mayer, Arizona. Most were former fairgrounds or racetracks, with minimal added facilities. Many of the people from Los Angeles, for example, were taken to the luxurious Santa Anita racetrack, but the horse stalls and tents in which they were housed, often for months, were hardly luxurious.

The assembly centers were run by the army directly, but because neither Secretary Stimson nor Chief of Staff Marshall wanted the responsibility for permanent custody, a new civilian agency, the War Relocation Authority (WRA), was created by a Presidential executive order on March 18. The WRA administered the ten permanent camps, known as relocation centers,

MAP 2
Relocation Centers, 1942–1946

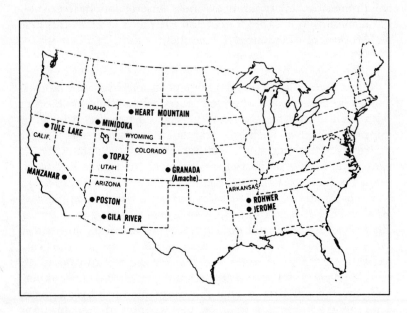

Source: Adapted from U.S. Department of War, *Final Report: Japanese Evacuation from the West Coast 1942* (Washington, D.C., 1943), Fig. 21, p. 257

which were "home" to some Japanese Americans until as late as March 1946. As its head, the President selected a scholarly New Deal bureaucrat from the Department of Agriculture, Milton S. Eisenhower, whose younger brother, Dwight, was then an obscure brigadier general on Marshall's staff. Unlike the army bureaucrats such as Gullion and Bendetsen, Milton Eisenhower and most of the New Dealers who ran the camps probably disapproved of them in principle and wanted to be "kindly keepers."

Eisenhower, in fact, originally planned to create something like "subsistence homesteads"—benign relief institutions established by the New Deal—in rural areas of the interior United States. He thought that these "would serve as staging areas" for the evacuees, most of whom "would be moved into private jobs as soon as possible." However, a meeting with Western governors in Salt Lake City early in April convinced him that such an enlightened policy was not politically feasible. As he reported in his memoirs—and a transcript of the meeting bears this out —the politicians objected vehemently.

> One governor shouted: "If these people are dangerous on the Pacific coast they will be dangerous here! We have important defense establishments, too, you know." Another governor [Nels Smith of Wyoming] walked close to me, shook his fist in my face, and growled through clenched teeth: "If you bring Japanese into my state, I promise you they will be hanging from every tree."

After this meeting, Eisenhower saw "no alternative to the unhappy one of creating evacuation camps where the people could live in modest comfort, do useful work, have schools for their small children, and thus retain as much self-respect as the horrible circumstances permitted." Shortly before the Salt Lake City meeting, he had written his former boss, Secretary of Agriculture Claude Wickard, that "when the war is over and we consider calmly this unprecedented migration of 120,000 people, we as Americans are going to regret the unavoidable injustices that may have been done." The WRA director continued in his job only until the middle of June 1942. Given his feelings about the whole process of incarceration, he might have repeated his warnings to Wickard in his letter of resignation to President Roosevelt, but he did not. "Good" bureaucrats don't disturb their bosses, and Eisenhower was continuing his public career as assistant director of the Office of War Information. Thus, he told the President that "public attitudes have exerted a strong influence in shaping the program and charting its direction. In a democracy this is unquestionably sound and proper." He even suggested that 15 to 20 percent of the Nisei and 50 percent of the Issei were not "loyal," and that those of either generation "who prefer the Japanese way of life" be sent to Japan. More positively, he did urge Roosevelt to make a strong public statement on behalf of the loyal Nisei, raise the token wages that inmates were paid for work done in camp, and ask Congress to enact a special program of postwar rehabilitation for those Japanese Americans allowed to remain in the country.

Eisenhower's attitude typified the way that former New Deal bureaucrats involved in the incarceration rationalized their actions. Eisenhower, his successor Dillon S. Myer, and many others would never have instituted such a program, considered themselves humanitarians, and looked down on blatant racists like Gullion and Bendetsen. But they were willing to execute the program, and, in the process, developed attitudes about "good" and "bad" Japanese Americans based on the extent to which the inmates cooperated with their oppressors.

From the point of view of their keepers, most Japanese Americans were "good" Japanese. As typified by the testimony of the JACL leadership, most of the detainees cooperated with both the army and the WRA. It was not necessary to have squads of soldiers or policemen fan out and round up those to be evacuated. Japanese Americans obediently appeared at the designated assembly points at the appointed times in the same orderly way that most of them lived their lives.

Such behavior seemed unremarkable in the 1940s and 1950s. Since the 1960s, when dissent and distrust of the government became accepted, many Americans, including younger Japanese Americans, have questioned the wartime behavior of the Nisei. They have asked: Why didn't the Japanese American people resist? Why did they go off to camp so meekly? The questions, though natural, are not realistic. The probable consequences of mass disobedience by persons identified with the hated Japanese enemy in wartime are dreadful to contemplate. Although, as more and more people are now doing, one can question the enthusiastic endorsement by the JACL leadership of everything the government did to the innocent Japanese Americans, there can be no doubt that its policy of compliance was the only sensible one.

Even in 1942, there was a handful of dissidents who dared to resist what was unquestionably governmental oppression. Their resistance was non-violent and in the best American tradition. A few resisters, like the Omuras, publicly challenged the notion of mass incarceration before it began. James Omura, in fact, moved to Denver while it was still possible to do so. Later a few Nisei caught up in the process of removal and incarceration challenged in the courts the constitutionality of the mass incarcerations, and hundreds of incarcerated Japanese Americans staged mass protests, violent and non-violent, against various government policies.

Four of the legal challenges to the government eventually reached the Supreme Court. They came from individual Nisei who lived in Washington, Oregon, and California. These people did not know each other and took action independently. Gordon K. Hirabayashi, a Quaker whose parents had converted to Christianity in Japan, was a senior at the University of Washington in 1942. Sometime in early 1942 he decided to bear witness against the whole evacuation. But his local attorney was inexperienced in appellate procedure, and Roger Baldwin of the American Civil Liberties Union (ACLU) cravenly withdrew promised legal support, so Hirabayashi's case only tested the curfew regulations of DeWitt's Proclamation No. 3. Hirabayashi was convicted in the Seattle Federal District Court and his appeal was decided by the Supreme Court in June 1943. *Hirabayashi v. US* (320 *US* 81) was decided in favor of the government, 9–0. Not a single Justice publicly opposed the racist policy of applying a curfew to only one ethnic group of the population. We now know that one Justice, Frank Murphy, wrote a dissent but, under pressure from his colleagues, modified it into a concurrence. In a strong statement which drew little notice at the time, Murphy insisted:

The broad provisions of the Bill of Rights . . . are not suspended by the mere existence of a state of war . . . Today is the first time, so far as I am aware, that we have sustained a substantial restriction of the personal liberty of citizens of the United States based on the accident of race or ancestry . . . It bears a melancholy resemblance to the treatment accorded to [Jews] in Germany.

But for Chief Justice Harlan F. Stone, who wrote the opinion, the issue was not Gordon Hirabayashi's civil rights but whether the United States had "the power to wage war successfully."

Stone swallowed whole the army's claim of military necessity presented to the Court by the Solicitor General. He also put his stamp of approval on racism.

> Because racial discriminations are in most circumstances irrelevant and therefore prohibited, it by no means follows that, in dealing with the perils of war, Congress and the Executive are wholly prohibited from taking into account those facts . . . which may in fact place citizens of one ancestry in a different category.

This latter statement disturbed Justice William O. Douglas, a New Deal liberal who, though he approved the decision, tried unsuccessfully to get the Chief Justice to remove the words about racial discrimination because it "implies or is susceptible to the inference that the Japs who are citizens cannot be trusted because we have treated them so badly."

A companion case, heard at the same time, involved the deliberate curfew violation of Minoru Yasui. A native of Oregon, Yasui was an attorney and a reserve officer in the U.S. Army through an ROTC commission. He was an employee of the Japanese consulate in Chicago, but resigned immediately after Pearl Harbor, returned home to Oregon, and tried, unsuccessfully, to go on active military duty. At his trial for curfew violation, the federal judge in Portland found him guilty, but by a different kind of reasoning. The judge in Seattle had merely accepted what the government had done. Judge James Alger Fee held that citizens could not be forced to obey DeWitt's curfew, but ruled that because of Yasui's employment by the Japanese government he had chosen "allegiance to the Emperor of Japan" and was therefore no longer an American citizen; thus, according to Fee, Yasui had to obey the curfew, since he was an "enemy alien." The Supreme Court did not rule on Yasui's case but ordered it returned to the Portland court and called the judge's attention to its decision in Hirabayashi's case. Judge Fee altered his ruling to comply with that of the highest court.

All the Hirabayashi case decided was that DeWitt's curfew order, under wartime circumstances, was legal. The other two

Japanese American cases, as they are called, dealt with persons who were actually in camps and called into question the whole policy of mass incarceration. They were decided together by the Supreme Court in December 1944, when there was no longer the slightest danger of a Japanese attack and American victory in the Pacific seemed assured. Fred T. Korematsu, unlike the other three litigants, did not deliberately challenge the law to provoke a test case. Instead of reporting for relocation, he went "underground"—actually, he was helping the war effort as a welder in a shipyard, under a Mexican name—but was soon turned in to the FBI. Arrested and awaiting trial, he was approached by a civil-liberties lawyer and agreed to challenge the constitutionality of the government's order. He was convicted in San Francisco's federal district court in September 1942, but his sentence was suspended and he was sent to a relocation center. His lawyers appealed, and *Korematsu v. US* (323 US 214) was finally decided by the Supreme Court in December 1944. The Court upheld Korematsu's conviction, 6–3, thus ratifying the legality of the incarceration of the Japanese Americans. The opinion was written by Hugo Black, the former Ku Klux Klan member from Alabama who had become a paladin of civil liberties. He insisted that racial prejudice had nothing to do with his decision.

> Regardless of the true nature of the assembly and relocation centers—and we deem it unjustifiable to call them concentration camps with all the ugly connotations that term implies—we are dealing specifically here with nothing but an exclusion order. To cast this case into outlines of racial prejudice, without reference to the real military dangers which were presented, merely confuses the issue. Korematsu was not excluded from the Military Area because of hostility to him or to his race.

Twenty-three years later, in an interview with *The New York Times* on September 2, 1971, Justice Black was unrepentant, telling the reporter in decidedly unjudicial language that there were lots of disloyal Japanese Americans who would have fought alongside any invading Japanese troops, and since "they all look alike to a person not a Jap," it would have been dangerous to leave any Japanese Americans at liberty.

Three Justices, all of whom had concurred in *Hirabayashi*, dissented. Owen J. Roberts, whose report on Pearl Harbor had provided arguments for those who favored incarceration, differentiated between the two cases: "This is not a case of keeping people off the streets at night . . . It is a case of convicting a citizen . . . for not submitting to imprisonment in a concentration camp solely because of his ancestry." Justice Robert Jackson, who as the chief American prosecutor at the international war-crimes trials at Nuremberg would soon make decisions about the legality of the actions of German generals, was unable to make a judgment about the actions of American generals. He said that there was no way for him to decide whether General DeWitt's orders were based on sound military judgment, and maintained that they might have been "permissible" though not "constitutional." The courts, Jackson argued, should not "have attempted to interfere with the Army" in 1942, but in 1944 things were different. If the Court now held that DeWitt's order was constitutional, Jackson said, "then we may as well say that any military order [in wartime] will be constitutional and have done with it." He would have found for Korematsu and ordered his immediate release. The third dissenter, Frank Murphy, argued that General DeWitt's orders went "over the brink of constitutional power" and that his brethren's approval of them constituted a "legalization of racism." He concluded with a ringing statement of cultural pluralism:

> All residents of this nation are kin in some way by blood and culture to a foreign land. Yet they are primarily and necessarily a part of this new civilization of the United States. They must accordingly be treated at all times as the heirs of the American experiment and as entitled to all of the rights and freedoms granted by the Constitution.

For all its candor and forthrightness, however, Murphy's dissent did not look behind DeWitt and see the Secretary of War, and, behind him, Franklin D. Roosevelt. The Roosevelt court did not often point accusing fingers at its creator, but surely Murphy understood that F.D.R.'s Executive Order 9066 was what gave DeWitt authority to act.

The fourth challenger was Mitsuye Endo, a civil servant of the state of California with brothers serving overseas in the United States Army. She had obeyed all of DeWitt's orders but from the start intended to make a test case. She contacted a civil-liberties attorney, James Purcell, who visited her in the horse stall at Tanforan where the army had put her. The strategy they decided on was to wait until she was shipped to a relocation center and then apply for a writ of habeas corpus, which, if granted, would give her immediate freedom. Although she had to wait for more than two years before her case, *Ex parte Endo* (323 US 283), was decided, she was victorious. A unanimous court restored her freedom.

Justice William O. Douglas's opinion, however, did not suggest that the President, the Congress, or even the army had done anything unconstitutional or improper when it ordered her to leave her home and incarcerated her. The villain, according to Douglas, was the civilian War Relocation Authority! "Whatever power the War Relocation Authority may have to detain other classes of citizens, it has no authority to [detain] citizens who are concededly loyal . . ." Both Murphy and Roberts, who agreed with the result, filed critical concurrences. Murphy again complained of "the unconstitutional resort to racism inherent in the entire evacuation program," while Roberts criticized the majority for ignoring the serious constitutional questions Endo's detention raised: "An admittedly loyal citizen has been deprived of her liberty for a period of years. Under the Constitution she should be free to come and go as she pleases."

Other Japanese Americans resisted oppression and confinement in different ways. There was some violence, most of it directed not against the authorities but against fellow Japanese Americans who, it was believed, were collaborating with the oppressive government. Such persons were usually called "inu," literally "dog," but in contemporary American slang "rat fink" would be a better translation. There were fatal riots at both California camps, Manzanar and Tule Lake, in which armed soldiers guarding the camps shot unarmed protesters to death. And at the camp at Topaz, Utah, a guard killed an old man who, the guard claimed, had tried to go through the fence.

Although most of the camps were peaceful most of the time, each was the scene of some kind of resistance. Perhaps most striking was the resistance to the military draft which was reapplied in January 1944 to all male Japanese American citizens of military age who had taken loyalty oaths. It was even applied to those who were still in concentration camps! (Many Nisei had been released by then.) An anti-draft movement began in the camp at Heart Mountain, Wyoming, where eighty-five of the inmates refused induction, maintaining that, as long as they and their parents were deprived of their liberty, they had no obligation to serve in the military. The federal government, with the support of the ACLU and other liberals, convicted the resisters and sent them to federal penitentiaries. But even at Heart Mountain, draft resistance was a minority phenomenon: 700 men there did go through the induction process, and 385 entered the army. At least eleven of the latter were killed in action, and fifty-two wounded. A total of 291 young men were tried for draft resistance in the camps, and 263 were convicted. 3,600 young men entered the army directly from the camps. At least 172 were killed in action; 590 were wounded, and fifteen were declared missing. Most of these—whether volunteers or draftees—served in the segregated 442nd Regimental Combat Team, which became the most decorated unit in the entire American Army. During prolonged combat in Italy and France, the 442nd and its predecessor unit from Hawaii, the 100th Battalion, suffered severe casualties and its men won 18,143 individual decorations, including a Congressional Medal of Honor, 47 Distinguished Service Crosses, 350 Silver Stars, and more than 3,600 Purple Hearts. The Congressional Medal of Honor, one of only twenty-nine awarded during the whole war, was awarded posthumously to Private First Class Sadao S. Munemori. In what may have been the supreme irony of their service, the men of the 442nd helped to liberate the Nazi concentration camp at Dachau even while their parents and other relatives were still held in American concentration camps.

But life behind barbed wire in America's concentration camps was not, in the main, a story of resistance or of heroism, but essentially one of survival. Most inmates did not actively resist. The issues that most people grappled with were how to make their lives more bearable, to what extent they should cooperate with their oppressors, and, finally, how and under what circumstances they would be able to leave camp. These basic problems split the incarcerated communities and even divided families. A simple chronological typology of life in the camps would run something like this:

PHASE I. Settling in (spring 1942–February 1943)
PHASE II. Registration/segregation crisis (February 1943–January 1944)
PHASE III. Draft crisis (January 1944–November 1945)
PHASE IV. Leaving camp (summer 1942–March 1946)

For most inmates, the settling-in process had to be accomplished twice: first at the army-run assembly centers; then, weeks or a couple of months later, at the WRA relocation centers.* The arrival at assembly centers was particularly traumatic. Most people had not known where they were being taken. All around the camps was dust, which became mud when it rained, and there was barbed wire, floodlights, and armed soldiers. Most, if not all, of the sites were overcrowded and not really prepared for human habitation. Toilet and bathing facilities were minimal. From the center in Merced, for example, one woman prisoner wrote:

> The lavatories [are] not very sanitary . . . The toilets are one big row of seats, that is, one straight board with holes out about a foot apart with no partitions at all and all the toilets flush together . . . about every five minutes. The younger girls couldn't go to them at first until they couldn't stand it any longer, which is really bad for them.

* The exceptions were most of those who went directly to Manzanar, which served as both an assembly center and a relocation center.

To make matters worse, improper sanitation in the makeshift mess kitchens caused mass outbreaks of diarrhea. The United States Public Health Service reported surprise that "so few epidemics have occurred from unsanitary conditions," and the army's own experts reported that kitchens were "not up to Army standards of cleanliness," that "bread and milk" were the only foods provided for small children, that dishwashing was not effective, due to "an insufficiency of hot water," and that there were "no cribs" for children in the improvised hospital. Inmates with money could supplement their diets from a kind of store set up by the army, but initially no one thought to stock items such as sanitary napkins. However, the prison-like assembly centers, for all their inadequacies, were largely in familiar territory, and the people in them could be visited by non-Japanese friends, though separated by barbed wire. Any presents brought had to be inspected by the guards.

The WRA camps, conversely, were at desolate, faraway sites where no one had lived before and no one has lived since. The army insisted that the camps all be at a "safe location" from what it called "strategic sites"—including any major highway or railroad line. None enjoyed a benign climate, and at some, weather conditions were brutally harsh. At Heart Mountain, Minidoka, and Topaz, winter temperatures of − 30F. and colder were not uncommon. Despite this, and though many were unfinished when the Japanese Americans first arrived, facilities at the WRA camps eventually were better than those in the assembly centers. At cold Heart Mountain, for example, the stoves were not all in place until sometime in November.

Each relocation center became a kind of American community, with many of the institutions that existed in the larger society. There were schools, libraries, hospitals, newspapers, churches, and what the WRA called "community government," which was really a way of getting inmates to do most of the housekeeping chores for a wage that could not exceed $19 a month, whether the worker was a janitor or one of the Japanese American physicians, nurses, and dentists upon whom the health of the detainees depended. No important decisions could be made by the so-called government.

Relocation had proceeded largely on a family basis: each

family had been assigned a number and tagged, like baggage, with that number during the move by the army. The number of family members determined the space each family was allocated in the relocation centers. Each was assigned what the WRA called an "apartment"—actually, a segment of one of the long, uniform barracks-like one-story buildings. At Topaz, which was representative, the uninsulated barracks were twenty feet wide. Thus, all "apartments" were twenty feet in one dimension: and as little as eight feet or as much as twenty-four feet in the other. The largest "apartment" was an unpartitioned area of twenty by twenty-four feet; that 480 square-foot space would be "home" for a family of six. Partitions between "apartments" did not reach the roof, so that privacy within or between family living spaces was impossible. As the camp populations declined, conditions improved somewhat. By April 1943 the average Topaz inmate had 114 square feet of living space; that is, an area six by nineteen feet.

No apartment had running water; eventually, all had electricity. Heating systems varied; most camps used coal stoves and most camp survivors remember that it was difficult to keep warm. Except for army-style cots, furniture was not supplied, and inmates had not been allowed to bring their own. Eventually, most made chairs and tables from scrap lumber or larger pieces "scrounged" from official building projects.

There were no individual cooking facilities. Everyone ate in the mess hall. Three times a day, prisoners lined up with trays to receive wholesome, starchy, cheap food, not usually prepared in the most appetizing manner. The army calculated that it spent 38.19 cents a day feeding each detainee in assembly centers; at the same time, the army spent 50 cents a day on its soldiers. The WRA probably spent a little more; in addition, the diet was often supplemented with vegetables grown by the camp inmates. Almost everyone complained about the food, but what the mess halls did to family relationships was worse. Youngsters tended to eat in groups and move around from mess hall to mess hall. The dislocation of the typical family meal was but another way in which the detention process eroded the dignity and authority of parents. Although the kindly keepers of the WRA claimed to have the interests of the Japanese

Americans at heart, none seems ever to have suggested that the government spend the money to provide kitchen facilities for individuals or for small groups.

Except at times of particular tension, boredom was a major fact of camp life; the phrase "waste time" became a kind of theme for teenagers. Yet, as Harry Kitano pointed out years ago, there was a positive side to the camp experience. For the first time the Nisei could fill a variety of social roles that had been closed to them in their home communities. Those in school became student-body leaders, captains of athletic teams, and editors of yearbooks. Those with teacher training could teach; others took on community leadership at an earlier age than would have been possible otherwise. And for some of the older people there was, for the first time in their adult lives, a great deal of leisure.

Then, just as the prisoners were adjusting to camp life, they were thrown into turmoil by the registration/segregation crisis. The crisis stemmed from an army decision announced by Secretary Stimson on January 28, 1943, that an all-Nisei combat team of perhaps five thousand men drawn from the mainland and Hawaii would be recruited. President Roosevelt praised the decision in a public statement which proclaimed that "Americanism is not, and never was, a matter of race or ancestry." The army prepared a questionnaire for male Japanese American citizens of military age—adapted from an existing questionnaire for aliens. The WRA, in a move of almost incredible stupidity, decided to have the questionnaire, which it retitled "Application for Leave Clearance," filled out by everyone over age seventeen, male or female, citizen or alien.

However their actions may appear today, WRA officials regarded themselves as enlightened liberals doing an unpleasant task as humanely as possible. A final report was called "A Story of Human Conservation," and certainly the Japanese Americans were better off under the WRA than they would have been in the hands of Provost Marshal General Gullion and his subordinates. The thrust of the WRA's registration plan may have been benign—the bureaucrats wanted to accelerate the movement of "loyal" Japanese Americans out of the camps—but the notion that a questionnaire was an appropriate way to test loyalty was foolish, as was having everyone fill it out. Had the questionnaire been restricted to citizens of military age—what the army wanted—and to those wishing to leave camp—what the WRA wanted—the damage would have been less severe. In any event, this crisis further divided the troubled community.

The crucial questions in the WRA's questionnaire were:

27. Are you willing to serve in the armed forces of the United States on combat duty, wherever ordered?
28. Will you swear unqualified allegiance to the United States of America and faithfully defend the United States from any or all attack by foreign or domestic forces, and foreswear any form of allegiance to the Japanese emperor, to any other foreign government, power or organization?

The inappropriateness of putting such questions to incarcerated enemy aliens or to women seems not to have occurred to anyone in the WRA until *after* the first questionnaires had been distributed. Question 28 was modified for aliens, but by then the damage had been done. There were objections from the community, all of whose members had good reason to mistrust the United States government. Some Nisei, for example, thought that question 28, which asked them to "foreswear" allegiance to Japan, was a trap designed to make them admit that they had previously had such an allegiance. Others qualified their answers to question 27 with phrases such as "Yes, if my rights as a citizen are restored." Many of the Issei, who feared that they would be thrown out of camp without resources if they said yes, answered no for that reason. Others were or had become loyal to Japan; for Issei to renounce Japanese nationality at a time when they could not become American citizens was to opt for statelessness.

Both the WRA and the JACL urged the Japanese to answer yes, and eventually most complied. Almost 75,000 of the nearly 78,000 camp residents over seventeen filled out questionnaires. About 6,700 answered no to question 28 and were therefore classified as disloyal by the WRA. Nearly two thousand others qualified their answers; almost all of these were recorded as disloyal as well. More than 65,000 persons, however, answered yes and went down in the WRA's books as loyal. One young

Nisei who said yes and actually volunteered for military service explained that [it was] "a hard decision . . . I know that this will be the only way that my family can resettle in [California] without prejudice or persecution."

Soon after the questionnaires were tabulated, the WRA decided that it would segregate the "loyal" from the "disloyal" by moving the latter to one camp, Tule Lake, California, and moving "loyal" Tuleans to other camps to replace them.* This split many families—often, but not always, along generational lines. It also meant, of course, that many minor children who were American citizens were taken to Tule Lake by alien parents. Eventually, Tule Lake filled with dissidents, became a strife-ridden camp, and was for a time turned over to the army in an attempt to quell the almost constant disorder there.

While the transfers necessitated by the segregation program were still going on, the draft was reinstituted for Japanese American citizens, both inside and outside of relocation centers. Draft eligibles who had answered no were usually not slated for induction. Thus, the draft resistance was restricted to men who had previously affirmed their loyalty. The arguments over this resistance—it was denounced by the JACL, the WRA, and the ACLU—sowed further bitterness in the community, not only against the government but also between Japanese Americans who supported the restoration of the draft and those who felt that it was just one more outrage perpetrated against an oppressed people.

These three crises—the fourth will be discussed in the following chapter—have dominated the literature about the camps. But the residents themselves were more often concerned with the problems of day-to-day living, of improving the way they lived, of getting an education, and, in some cases, of preparing for eventual release. Many of those who were employed, particularly those with responsible or absorbing jobs, made those jobs the focus of their lives. Many found consolation in religion, and both Christian and Buddhist services were held regularly. Others concentrated on hobbies; still others sought self-improvement

---

* It is possible that the WRA leadership had always intended that segregation follow registration.

by taking adult classes, ranging from Americanization and American history and government to vocational courses in secretarial skills and bookkeeping, and cultural courses in such things as ikebana, Japanese flower arrangement. The young people spent much time in recreational pursuits: news of sports, theatricals, and dances fills the pages of the camp newspapers.

There were so many of these "normal" activities that some imagined that the nine "regular" relocation centers were like other American communities. This, unfortunately, was not the case. The barbed-wire fences, the guards, and the surrounding wasteland were always there to remind the detainees that they were exiled, incarcerated Americans, who didn't know whether they would ever be allowed to return to their former homes.

4

RETURN TO FREEDOM,

1942–1946

PUTTING the Japanese Americans into camps took only a few months, but getting them all out again took almost four years. Contrary to popular belief, the process of leaving camp started almost immediately, in the summer of 1942, and continued even as the camps were filling up. Although more than 120,000 individuals were held in relocation centers at one time or another, the camp population peaked at a little over 107,000 in the winter of 1943. By the beginning of the following year, it was down to 93,000, and by January 1, 1945, before the liberating effects of the Endo decision kicked in, it had dropped to just under 80,000. At the beginning of August 1945, the month when the war with Japan ended, there were fewer than 58,000 inmates. By December 1, 1945, every camp but Tule Lake had been emptied: there were 12,545 detainees still there; and as late as March 1, 1946, it still held 2,806.

In 1942 four separate groups of Japanese Americans were quietly released from camps; the government had a different rationale for each. The first to be approved for release were college students. The impetus for their release came from West Coast educators. Robert Gordon Sproul, president of the University of California, led the way. Sproul assumed that the evacuation was "a necessary evil" and believed that "the efforts we expend now will be repaid a thousandfold in the attitude of citizens of Japanese ancestry in years to come." In addition, he thought that in the new and better [post-war] world . . . our handling of this serious minority group problem will be looked upon [by foreigners] as evidence of our intentions and a proof of the ideals to which we hold.

The feelings of Sproul and a number of other California university presidents were presented before California Governor Culbert Olson, who sent a letter to President Roosevelt in late April stating that,

unless some special action is taken, the education of those who might become influential leaders of the loyal American born Japanese will abruptly be closed. Such a result would be injurious not only to them, but to the nation, since well trained leadership for such persons will be needed after the present war.

There was some debate within the Administration about the wisdom of releasing any Japanese Americans, even students of unquestioned loyalty, but in part due to the influence of White House advisor Harry L. Hopkins, the educators' proposal carried the day. In mid-May 1942, Roosevelt wrote Olson that, before the fall semester began, "qualified American-born Japanese students will be enabled to continue their education in inland institutions," and assured the governor that Milton Eisenhower and his "Japanese Relocation Authority" [sic] would make satisfactory arrangements. Eisenhower established a committee chaired by Clarence E. Pickett, head of the Quaker American Friends Service Committee, to advise the War Relocation Authority on the best way to accomplish this.

Many American institutions of higher learning, including some of the most prestigious, such as Princeton and MIT, refused to admit Japanese American students in 1942, but other colleges and universities did. In general, private schools were more receptive than public institutions. Eventually, some 4,300 students were released from government camps to go to college. The student pioneers were counseled by the WRA to keep a low profile, and most tried to do so. As one wrote back from the University of Nebraska, where Asian faces were a novelty, "all of us have tried to avoid being seen in conspicuous groups and have tried to spread out as much as possible."

There were inevitable setbacks. At the University of Idaho, for example, community pressure caused the school to rescind the admission of six Nisei in the fall of 1942. Conditions were so tense that two young women were kept in jail under "protective custody." In the following academic year, when hysteria had abated, Nisei students were again admitted to the University of Idaho. Despite threatening incidents, most Japanese American students reported that they were well treated and most excelled academically.

If the long-term goals of democracy were being served by releasing students, the freeing of the other three groups of inmates served more mundane purposes. Wartime prosperity had made it even harder than usual for Western growers to get the temporary help that their "factories in the field" required at harvest time, and the incarcerated Japanese Americans seemed an ideal labor force. Thus, in late May 1942, a first group of fifteen were temporarily allowed to leave the Portland, Oregon, Assembly Center to thin sugar beets in the southeastern corner of Oregon, some miles outside of DeWitt's prohibited zone. They were housed in a Farm Security Administration camp at Nyssa. By June, "about a hundred Japanese" from Portland and other assembly centers were working there. One man described the working and living conditions favorably, but noted a basic anomaly:

> The camp is on a self-governing basis except for one camp manager. We are required to be in the camp area between the hours of 8:00 P.M. and 6:00 A.M. There are no restrictions on lights-out, no guards, no fence but you cannot go out of camp unless accompanied by some [government] official or your employer. Other Japanese residing in the same vicinity have no restrictions whatsoever.

Eventually, some ten thousand people were released from camps to do agricultural work during 1942 alone. About half of them went to the fields from assembly centers and entered relocation centers only after their harvest work was done. While the vast majority of these releases were temporary, some were permanent. There is no record of any attempted escapes by those on temporary release. Like the college students, they encountered much animosity and some violence, most frequently in the form of stone throwing. The worst violence occurred at a farm labor camp in Utah one night in October 1943, when fifteen to eighteen shots were fired into lighted buildings, wounding three Nisei, none seriously. Despite such harassment, most Japanese were glad to be out of camp and earning more than $19 a month. Secretary of the Interior Harold L. Ickes publicly extolled the release policy, telling *The New York Times* in mid-June 1942:

> I do not like the idea of loyal citizens, whatever their race or color, being kept in relocation centers any longer than need be . . . We need competent help very badly and these are highly skilled workers.

These workers, and those who harvested crops in subsequent years, made significant contributions to the American economy and to the war effort. The Utah–Idaho Sugar Company, for example, hired some 3,500 evacuees in 1942. The economic historian Leonard Arrington has shown that the company's large-scale use of Japanese American labor resulted in almost 100 million pounds of additional sugar produced in 1942 alone and that those released from the camps "were among the most industrious and intelligent workmen who ever labored in the region." There was an irony in this use of Japanese American labor at the typically low wages that prevailed even in wartime agriculture. Had they been left in California and other coastal regions, many of these same workers would have been running their own farms, reaping wartime profits, and hiring others, at low wages, to help them do so.

The third group was set free by the United States Army— not, to be sure, by the Western Defense Command, but by the army nevertheless. Japanese linguists were desperately needed by the military. The army had established its language school —the forerunner of today's Defense Language Institute—at the

Presidio in San Francisco early in 1941, and its faculty included some civilian Japanese American instructors who taught Japanese. General DeWitt insisted that the school either get rid of its Japanese American personnel or get out of California: as the school could not function without a Japanese American faculty, it moved to Minnesota in midwinter, much to the annoyance of its officers. By July its commandant, Danish-born Lieutenant Colonel Kai E. Rasmussen, had gotten special authority from the War Department to send recruiting teams into the camps to find linguistically qualified persons who were willing to volunteer for service in military intelligence. General DeWitt and his staff protested against this policy but were unable to stop the recruiting.

The language-school officials hoped to find Kibei—Nisei who had been sent to Japan for part of their education—who had been non-commissioned officers in the Japanese military, since such men would be familiar with Japanese military terms and usage. They did not find even one such person; in fact, their expectations about the linguistic abilities of the American-born Japanese were inflated. Most Nisei, like most other second-generation Americans, had little facility in the language of their parents, and most of what they did know was "baby talk," what they had learned to say to their parents. One account indicated that, of the first 3,700 Nisei interviewed, only 3 percent spoke Japanese fluently, another 4 percent could be considered fairly proficient, while another 3 percent knew just enough to make their training seem worthwhile. Journalist-historian Bill Hosokawa describes his interview by Rasmussen:

> I thought I [had] a fair speaking knowledge of the language, but he quickly proved me completely inadequate . . . First he asked me to read a high-school text. I could make out perhaps two or three characters in a hundred.

Finally, with what the journalist remembered as "ill-concealed disgust," the commandant rejected him, remarking: "Hosokawa, you'd make a helluva Jap."

Eventually, language-school standards were lowered, and some six thousand volunteer and drafted Japanese Americans attended the Military Intelligence Specialist School. About five thousand of its Japanese American graduates were sent overseas to various parts of the Pacific Theater of Operations. Some served in headquarters units; others, with combat units such as Merrill's Marauders in the jungles of Burma. They translated captured documents, monitored radio traffic, and otherwise used their linguistic skills to help defeat the nation from which their parents had come. Their Japanese faces made them potential targets of their fellow American soldiers, so they often did their work with armed military bodyguards. Unlike the well-publicized efforts of the Japanese American fighters in Italy and France, the valor of the Japanese military-intelligence specialists received almost no publicity.

And, finally, some men and women from the WRA camps were included on each of the two trips of the Swedish liner *Gripsholm* to exchange Japanese and American diplomats and other civilians that one government was willing to release and the other was willing to accept. Most of the more than two thousand sent to Japan were either diplomats or persons interned in the camps of the Immigration and Naturalization Service, but a minority came from the relocation centers. Many more of the Issei wanted to return to Japan than could be accommodated on the vessel, but a proposed third exchange never materialized. The issue of repatriation and/or exile to Japan would arise again in the aftermath of the registration/segregation crisis of 1943.

The impetus for the release of each of these groups came from outside the War Relocation Authority, although the WRA willingly cooperated. The educators who fostered the college program for the Nisei had wanted the students to be subsidized by the U.S. Office of Education. That funding never materialized, and most students were helped with private scholarships. The WRA was able to provide a travel allowance and a modest grant—usually $25 a person—for the students, a policy that was continued for others being resettled. Both the original WRA head, Milton Eisenhower, and his successor, Dillon S. Myer, who ran the agency from June 1942 until its dissolution in March 1946, favored the release of "loyal" Japanese Americans as quickly as possible. Both men believed that there were significant numbers of "disloyal" persons in each generation, however, and they combined their plans for resettling Japanese Americans in the interior with loyalty oaths.

The first permanent resettlement began in late September 1942, when Myer announced new WRA regulations effective October 1. The WRA called its release policy "leave clearance" and pretended that it maintained some kind of control over released inmates, but it did not. Its final report showed that it had released more than 2,300 persons without even being aware of their destination. Only after the Endo decision in December 1944 did the agency speak of release. At first, only Nisei could apply, but the procedure was later broadened to include Issei. Historian Sandra C. Taylor has described the process, aptly, as "cumbersome, tedious and time consuming." "Leave clearance" involved a great deal of paperwork, clearance by the FBI—not an investigation but a mere checking of each applicant's name against lists of putatively dangerous Japanese. Only *after* mass evacuation and incarceration had appeased the public and the politicians was the executive branch willing to assess the loyalty of the Japanese Americans. Reversing the usual American assumption, they were presumed guilty until demonstrated innocent.

To facilitate resettlement, the WRA opened six regional offices and thirty-five sub-regional offices across the United States whose purpose was to prepare both the receiving community for the Japanese and the Japanese for the receiving community. In the camps, the WRA gave briefings and provided specific information about particular cities; in the cities, it set up committees of volunteers from civic and religious groups to ease possible tensions. In addition, hostels run by Quakers and other religious groups were established in many cities to provide temporary homes for those being resettled. Workers and housing were both in short supply during the war, and the Japanese Americans had a much easier time getting jobs than finding suitable places to live.

For those who were educationally and psychologically equipped to take advantage of it, resettlement was an advantage. Not only did it get these people out of camp, but it enabled many to break out of the restrictive employment patterns that had prevailed on the Pacific Coast. This is well described in a letter one resettled Nisei wrote from Chicago to President Sproul:

> Hundreds of Japanese Americans are employed in occupations which were denied to them on the Pacific Coast. They have, for the first time, found occupational outlets . . . As you well know a great many Japanese Americans graduated from institutions of higher learning but were pigeon-holed into narrow employment channels.

Of the nearly 30,000 traceable persons who resettled from relocation centers before January 1, 1945, more than 75 percent were in just eight states. Illinois led with 7,652 (6,599 in Chicago), followed by Colorado, 3,185; Ohio, 2,854; Utah, 2,427; Idaho, 2,084; Michigan, 1,990; Minnesota, 1,292; and New York, 1,131. The appeal of the Midwest is clear. New York City's traditional attraction for migrants was dampened both by the WRA's reluctance to have the Japanese settle on the seaboard and by a stream of anti-Japanese remarks from Mayor Fiorello La Guardia. Colorado, Utah, and Idaho drew resettlers because they had relocation camps in them and nearby locations offered employment opportunities. In Utah, for example, the Tooele Ordnance Depot began hiring Nisei from the Topaz camp in late 1942; by the end of the war, some 250 were employed there. How persons who were so dangerous to national security that they had to be moved out of their homes and locked up could be trusted to work in a munitions factory is something the government never tried to explain.

A brief glance at Cincinnati, Ohio, where more than six hundred Japanese Americans settled, illustrates the process. G. Raymond Booth, the WRA official there, made the following pitch for Ohio's Queen City in the Rohwer, Arkansas, camp newspaper in May 1943. Cincinnati, he said, was

> a good place for evacuees to relocate in. Japanese faces are not unknown here. There have been a few since the Centennial Fair of 1888 including two brilliant and honored scientists at the University of Cincinnati . . . There are some

100 job offerings waiting to be accepted now. Some of them are quite good . . . Those who come here may confidently start putting down their roots.

A week later, a former Rohwer inmate wrote in the same camp paper:

We have found a place where we can start to build and plan for the future . . . Cincinnati has given us an impression of kindliness . . .

To be sure, these were propaganda documents. But most resettlers seemed to do relatively well in their new environments, and, of course, any free environment would have been an improvement over the camps.

Both the WRA and President Roosevelt hoped that the resettlement of small groups of Japanese Americans in places like Cincinnati would break up the prewar patterns of "clustering" on the Pacific Coast and that, once released from captivity, Japanese Americans would become more evenly distributed across the country. President Roosevelt had supported resettlement in September 1943, when he told the Senate that there were many Japanese Americans "whose loyalty to this country has remained unshaken through the hardships of the evacuation which military necessity made unavoidable." When questioned, at a November 21, 1944, press conference, about the possible return of Japanese Americans to the West Coast, Roosevelt deliberately evaded the question but noted:

A good deal of progress has been made in scattering them through the country, and that is going on every day . . . The example I always cite, to take a unit, is the . . . county . . . in [which] probably half a dozen or a dozen families could be scattered around on the farms and worked into the community.

After all, they are American citizens, and we all know that American citizens have certain privileges . . . 75,000 families scattered around the United States is not going to upset anybody . . . And, of course, we are actuated . . . by the very wonderful record that the Japanese in that battalion in Italy have been making in the war. It is one of the outstanding battalions that we have.

One of the rights that Japanese Americans did not yet have was the right to return to their homes in California and the forbidden areas of Washington, Oregon, and Arizona. The Supreme Court's December 1944 decision in the Endo case lifted that ban for Nisei not charged with disloyalty and thus changed the pattern of resettlement. Of the nearly 75,000 persons who left WRA camps after January 1, 1945, just over two-thirds went to the three West Coast states: 43,581 to California, 10,077 of them to Los Angeles; 4,471 to Washington; and 2,088 to Oregon. This was not the kind of scattering that the authorities wanted, but the 1950 census did show a reduction in the concentration of Japanese Americans on the Pacific Coast. Only 69.3 percent of mainland Japanese Americans lived in the three West Coast states in 1950, well below the prewar concentration of 88.5 percent.

The resettlers created new and permanent Japanese American communities far from the West Coast. The largest of these were in Chicago, Denver, Salt Lake City, and New York City. In such places there was no ethnic economy for them to work in and few ethnic institutions to shape their lives. While there were sometimes neighborhood clusters of Japanese Americans, there were no real ethnic enclaves, the Nihonmachi (Japan towns) which had been the centers of the Japanese American prewar communities. The Japanese Americans in the Midwest and East were certainly not fully integrated into the larger American society—and are not so today—but the minuscule size of the resettled populations meant that interaction with whites increased greatly. In the most populous new community, in Chicago, there were in 1950 only 11,000 Japanese Americans in a population of over two million.

There are many reasons for the relatively high degree of acceptance of Japanese Americans east of the Sierra Nevadas in wartime and postwar America. Once the initial shock wore off—resettler after resettler reported more stares of curiosity than of hostility—it became apparent to most of the other

Americans that the Nisei were hardworking, culturally conservative people with essentially middle-class aspirations and behavior patterns. In some cities, such as Chicago, it was probably just as important that they were not African Americans, against whom most white Chicagoans were extremely prejudiced. In addition, the Nisei image was helped by the positive "information campaign" of the WRA and the government propaganda agency, the Office of War Information. This propaganda stressed not only the American ideal of equality and the good citizenship of the resettlers but also the superb performance of the Japanese American troops fighting in Italy and southern France, a performance that was repeatedly praised by officials from the White House down. There was, to be sure, the usual anti-Japanese-American propaganda as well, mainly from two traditional opponents, organized labor and the American Legion and other veterans' organizations, but it was largely drowned out by voices calling for greater ethnic and racial equality. Although the term "model minority" was not coined until 1966, the seeds of the concept were planted in the waning years of World War II.

While the resettlers were pioneering on what were, for Japanese Americans, largely new urban frontiers, those back in camp—still the majority—were wracked by new crises and divisions. The departure of the resettlers had taken from the camps most of the more acculturated Nisei. Sandra Taylor, in her study of resettlement, notes that it was primarily young people between the ages of seventeen and thirty-five who took advantage of the resettlement. This meant that the camps increasingly held a higher proportion of older adults and small children, of Issei rather than Nisei. Pro-Japanese activity increased, as the relatively small minority of those who were actively loyal to Japan—many of whom had been "turned off" America by their unfair treatment—met less and less opposition within the camp population. There was much intimidation by a minority of aggressive young men, and not a little violence, almost all of it directed at "pro-American" inmates.

The WRA's answer to this was to initiate the policy it called "segregation," putting all the "disloyals" in one camp, Tule Lake, and transferring "loyals" from Tule Lake to other camps. Many of the leaders of the Japanese American community welcomed the segregation program, in part because they felt that it would highlight the loyalty of the majority. WRA administrators, other government officials, and JACL leaders all assumed that being "pro-American" or "pro-Japanese" was a simple matter of loyalty, like a true/false examination. Studies of Tule Lake, beginning with the famous wartime investigation by Dorothy S. Thomas and Richard S. Nishimoto, have shown that the situation was much more complex. First of all, the instrument used to determine loyalty, the questionnaire, was fatally flawed. In addition, many factors entered into individual decisions: whether to move to Tule Lake, whether to leave or to remain. The desire to keep the family together, a reluctance to move again, and resentment and disillusionment were often as significant as "loyalty" and "disloyalty." The following contemporary comments, recorded at Tule Lake by Thomas and Nishimoto and their informants, give a notion of the kinds of reasons, other than loyalty to Japan, that motivated some of the inmates to make their decisions.

An Issei man, aged forty-one, said that he didn't fill out the loyalty question at all—which meant that the government counted him as disloyal—because he feared that everyone who said yes would be forced to leave camp, and he had no place to go. Two American-born brothers, aged twenty and twenty-three, said: "We'd like to sit in Tule Lake for a while. We don't want to relocate. The discrimination is too bad." A young Nisei mother explained:

> I have American citizenship. It's no good, so what's the use? . . . I feel that we're not wanted in this country any longer. Before the evacuation I had thought that we were Americans, but our features are against us.

Eventually, more than 18,000 Japanese Americans were segregated at Tule Lake; almost a third of these were family members rather than the segregated themselves. Another third were old Tuleans: their motivation was like that of the Issei who stated:

Tuleans who are staying are often doing so because they didn't want to move. Those who are coming in here are among the worst because they wouldn't bother to pack and come here unless they were fairly bad.

Not surprisingly, after late 1943, when the transfers were completed, the Tule Lake camp became a trouble spot and for a time was turned over to the army and placed under martial law as vehemently pro-Japanese strong-arm squads terrorized fellow captives by insisting that all "true" Japanese would initiate requests for repatriation or expatriation to Japan. More than a third of the Tule Lake population—7,222 persons—formally applied to be sent to Japan. About 65 percent of those who did so were American-born, including the Nisei mother quoted above. The pro-Japanese minority within Tule Lake eventually demanded what it called "resegregation"; that is, that the majority of inmates—those who were still in Tule Lake but had not asked to be sent to Japan—be sent out of Tule Lake.

The WRA and the Department of Justice then took the next step: they asked Congress to make it easier for American citizens to renounce their citizenship. Congress, which constantly criticized both agencies as being "too soft on Japs," happily complied with the Denaturalization Act of 1944.

Edward J. Ennis, the Justice Department official who told interviewers in the 1980s that he wept when his Aliens Division had to collaborate with the army in its roundup of Japanese Americans in 1942, helped formulate the denaturalization policy. As he explained the Department's rationale at the time:

1. It feared that the courts might eventually declare continued detention of American citizens unconstitutional, and wanted some way to hold on to the "disloyals."
2. It feared that militant "disloyals," if released, would be dangerous.
3. It hoped that the bill would induce militant disloyals to renounce their citizenship and that they then could be detained no matter what the court did, because there was no dispute about the government's right to detain enemy aliens.

During the war, a total of 5,766 Americans of Japanese ancestry formally renounced their citizenship, and a large number of non-citizen Issei applied for repatriation. After the war, as soon as transportation was available, the American government began shipping Japanese Americans to Japan. A total of 4,724 persons were actually sent there from WRA camps. Of these, 1,659 were aliens; 1,949 were American citizens, mostly minors accompanying repatriating parents; and 1,116 were adult Nisei. More of those who had renounced their citizenship would have been sent to Japan had it not been for the San Francisco civil-liberties attorney Wayne Collins, who waged virtually a one-man legal campaign to regain citizenship for those who had renounced it. Some of the cases dragged on until 1968, and for a time these people had a unique status: they were, in the words of Donald Collins—no relation to Wayne—"native American aliens." The federal courts, with the reluctant consent of the Justice Department, ruled that acts of renunciation signed behind barbed wire were, in essence, made under duress and therefore null and void. A majority of the renunciants—including many of those who were sent to Japan —have probably regained their American citizenship.

The final crises for the incarcerated Japanese came in 1945 and early 1946 and involved the emptying of the camps and the return to the West Coast. The Endo decision, which mandated the reopening of the West Coast to "loyal" Japanese Americans, did not result in an immediate quickening of the pace of resettlement.* In fact, the resettlement rate was lower in the first three months of 1945 than it had been during most of 1944. With the West Coast open, fewer wished to go East, but most were naturally cautious about returning to their former homes. A group of Seattle hotelkeepers in the camp at Minidoka, for example, financed one of their number to return to their home town and bring back a firsthand report. He reported that there was much anti-Japanese hostility in Seattle, and some

* A few Japanese Americans, mostly members of interracial families, had been allowed to return to the West Coast earlier by the Western Defense Command. Before January 1, 1945, 194 Japanese had resettled in California.

hotelkeepers delayed returning. Despite bad reports and a number of instances of terrorism, mostly in rural California, the rate of West Coast resettlement began to pick up and by April 1945 was proceeding at a faster clip than at any previous time, and increased steadily thereafter. Yet, when the end of the war with Japan came, on August 14, 1945, more than a third of the exiled people—about 44,000 persons—were still in camps.

Even before the war ended, the WRA was phasing itself out. Jerome, one of the two camps in Arkansas, was closed in June 1944. In February 1945, the agency held an "all-center" conference of representatives of inmates of seven centers in Salt Lake City—no one was brought from the two camps in California—and JACL leaders to explain its closing policies. The agency announced its intention to close all camps within six to twelve months after the end of the war. In fact, it was able to do so in eight. The policy announcement had a seemingly paradoxical result: the representatives of the inmates and the JACL officials opposed closing the camps! They felt that many of the inmates had been so impaired by their captivity and by the loss of their assets that they would not be able to live on their own.

They wanted the WRA to stay in business indefinitely and be prepared to accept responsibility for those of the exiles who, for reasons of age, infirmity, or demoralization, were not prepared to return to freedom. The inmate representatives recommended that resettlers be given financial assistance, including lump-sum grants and long-term, low-interest loans, measures that the New Deal had instituted for all Americans during the Depression and which the federal government would reinstate in the 1950s and later, for various foreign refugees from Communism. The WRA rejected all these recommendations. There would be no special aid package for the returning exiles, and those who did not leave camp voluntarily by the deadline would be given the standard relocation allowance—$25 for individuals, $50 for families—and train fare back to the place from which they had been evacuated. Those who left voluntarily had a choice of destination. All the camps but Tule Lake were closed down by December 1945, and even it evicted the last inmate in March 1946. As the WRA itself commented, "the Government placed the remaining evacuees under direct compulsion to leave."

The WRA liked to think of its efforts in resettling the Japanese Americans and improving their image as "a story of human conservation." Certainly, the splendid recovery that many Japanese Americans made after their release gives some credence to that claim. It must not be forgotten, however, that thousands of Japanese Americans had their lives destroyed and were never able, for one reason or another, to recover. There can be no more poignant evidence of that human waste and of man's inhumanity to man than the fact that thousands of exiles, persons who had been part of a free and self-supporting community, were so shattered by their wartime treatment at the hands of their own government that they literally had to be evicted from concentration camps.

5

REHABILITATION AND
REDRESS, 1943–1990

EVEN as most Japanese Americans were still incarcerated in sand-and-cactus concentration camps, the first steps were being taken to reverse long-standing legal discrimination on a federal level aimed at Asians, discrimination that had begun with the Naturalization Act of 1870, which deliberately excluded Asians from those who could be naturalized. In 1943, as a gesture of friendship to a beleaguered wartime ally, the United States Congress, at President Roosevelt's request, repealed all or part of the fifteen separate statutes which had effected Chinese exclusion, gave what it called "persons of the Chinese race" a quota of 105 persons per year, and made "Chinese persons or persons of Chinese descent" eligible for naturalization on the same terms as other aliens. Just as the enactment of Chinese Exclusion in 1882 was the first evidence that the golden door of American immigration was closing, its repeal sixty-one years later was the first evidence that the doors were swinging open again. In 1946, Filipinos and natives of India were made eligible for immigration and naturalization. At last, in 1952, the otherwise reactionary McCarran–Walter act, passed over Harry Truman's veto, erased the final ethnic and racial bars to immigration and naturalization, so that other Asians, including Japanese, could become naturalized citizens. Surviving Issei became naturalized as rapidly as possible.

State laws discriminating against Asian Americans were also disappearing. In California, for example, what was left of the anti-Japanese coalition got a referendum put on the ballot in 1948 which proposed making the alien land acts more stringent.

The voters defeated it overwhelmingly: 59 percent voted against it. It was the first time an anti-Asian measure had lost in California. Soon after that, a variety of state laws such as the so-called anti-miscegenation statutes, which barred interracial marriages, and the hated alien land acts, were tossed on the legislative scrap heap.

Also in 1948, the federal government took its first step toward redress for the losses suffered by the Japanese American community. Except for radios, firearms, explosives, and fishing boats, the federal government had not confiscated Japanese American property. But since the Japanese Americans were deprived of both their liberty and their income, many lost farms and homes simply because they could no longer keep up their payments. President Truman, who had held a special ceremony on the ellipse behind the White House to award a Presidential Unit Citation to the Nisei 442nd Regimental Combat Team— "You have fought against prejudice and you have won," the President said—encouraged Congress to pass what became the Japanese American Claims Act of 1948. In the words of the Senate Report:

> The question of whether the evacuation of the Japanese people from the West Coast was justified is now moot. The Government did move these people, bodily, the resulting loss was great, and the principles of justice and responsible government require that there should be compensation for such losses.

The Claims Act, although important symbolically, was palpably inadequate as a financial settlement for losses of real property, which was all that it covered. Congress eventually appropriated just $38 million to satisfy some 23,000 claims totaling $131 million. The Department of Justice moved with almost glacial slowness. Bill Hosokawa reported that the government spent over a thousand dollars in fighting one $450 claim. After seventeen years of litigation, during which most claims were settled for a few cents on the dollar, the final claim was adjudicated in 1965.

No one knows the real worth of the property lost by the

Japanese Americans. As economists have pointed out, the true losses should take into account not just the 1942 value of the property but also the lost economic opportunities in a time when most Americans were enjoying wartime prosperity, and the tremendous increase in land values on the Pacific Coast. In addition, it must be remembered that the West Coast Issei were the only immigrant group in American history who had to get established twice, and many were simply too old and too discouraged to do so the second time.

Further evidence of the changing climate of opinion toward Asians is seen in the 1959 admission of Hawaii to statehood. Congress had long resisted this move, largely because the islands' polyglot population had a "non-white" majority. As Representative John E. Rankin (D-Miss.) remarked to Ernest Gruening, an official of the Department of the Interior, during a 1937 statehood hearing in the islands: "My God, if we give them folks statehood we're likely to have a senator called Moto."* Statehood has meant that Hawaii regularly sends Asian American legislators to Washington, and while the presence of three Japanese American senators and four Japanese American congressmen in the 96th Congress, which passed the law that eventually led to redress payments to the survivors of the incarceration, did not ensure its passage, it is impossible to imagine such an enactment without their input and influence.

In 1976, as part of the bicentennial celebration of the American Revolution, President Gerald R. Ford used the thirty-fourth anniversary of F.D.R.'s Executive Order 9066 to issue a proclamation repealing it. Insisting that "an honest reckoning" had to examine "national mistakes" as well as "national achievements," the President declared:

> We all know now what we should have known then—not only was that evacuation wrong, but Japanese Americans were and are loyal Americans. On the battlefield and at home, Japanese Americans—names like Hamada, Mitsu-

* During the 1930s and early 1940s, books and films about a fictional Japanese detective, Mr. Moto, created by John P. Marquand, were quite popular. Gruening's diary rendered Rankin's remarks in Southern dialect; that is, "Mah Gawd." I have put them into standard English.

mori, Marimoto, Noguchi, Yamasaki, Kido, Munemori, and Miyamura—have been and continue to be written into our history for the sacrifices and contributions they have made to the well-being and security of this, our common nation.*

In addition, on his last day in office, Ford issued a Presidential pardon for Iva I. Toguri, known as Tokyo Rose. Toguri had been convicted of treason for making wartime broadcasts from Tokyo in a 1949 trial during which, as legal historian Stanley I. Kutler has demonstrated, witnesses against her were allowed to present testimony that the federal prosecutors knew was perjured.

It was Ford's successor, Jimmy Carter, who helped begin the last phase of what Japanese Americans call the struggle for redress. In late 1980, Congress and the President created the Commission on the Wartime Relocation and Internment of Civilians (CWRIC). The Relocation Commission's mandate was to determine whether any wrong had been done to Japanese Americans during World War II, and if so, to recommend appropriate remedial action to the Congress. Thus, after almost forty years, the final act of the wartime ordeal of Japanese Americans unfolded. Although in one sense that ordeal began when President Franklin D. Roosevelt signed Executive Order 9066 on February 19, 1942, in another sense the ordeal goes back to the beginnings of anti-Asian sentiment on the West Coast of the United States in the mid-nineteenth century.

The redress movement—the term that Japanese Americans and their supporters use to describe their struggle for official recognition that a grievous wrong was done to them—had its origins in the early 1970s when a few activists in the Japanese American community began to call for redress, a call that almost all established community leaders either ignored or rejected outright. Many of these leaders had refused to support the tiny minority of Japanese Americans who publicly protested their incarceration during World War II. When President Ford, on the anniversary of the original order and as part of the bicentennial of the Constitution, revoked 9066 and hailed Japanese

* For the complete text, see Document 3.

American loyalty, many argued that redress had been accomplished. But others in the Japanese American community demanded a fuller form of redress: some would have settled for a formal apology from Congress; others wanted a more traditional form of redress, monetary compensation; and still others wanted both.

Community reactions and agendas were mixed. My own quite "unscientific" notion—"unscientific" because I conducted no poll—is that the division of opinion about redress within the Japanese American community was much like the division of opinion John Adams analyzed in 1776 with reference to the Declaration of Independence and its consequences: perhaps a third approved of it, another third opposed it, and the remainder was not much concerned one way or another. But pressures for action grew and finally affected the community's major organization, the Japanese American Citizens' League (JACL), which called for an apology and a cash payment, during its 1978 convention in Salt Lake City. The amount the JACL asked for —$25,000 to each individual who had been incarcerated— effectively set an upper-limit on what Japanese Americans might expect to receive.

The reasons for the opposition to the proposal within the Japanese American community were quite varied. Some, like Senator S. I. Hayakawa (R-Calif.), objected on ideological grounds. Calling it "absurd and ridiculous," he and others saw redress as another facet of the welfare state, which they generally opposed. But, as critics were quick to point out, the Canadian-born Hayakawa had spent the war in Chicago and had never been relocated or sent to a concentration camp. Some opponents of redress maintained that monetary payments could in no way wipe out the degradation they had experienced during the war. Others in the community favored redress but were outraged that the JACL had asked for so little. Many of these eventually joined a quixotic class-interest suit initiated by the newly formed, Chicago-based National Committee for Japanese American Redress, led by William Hohri. Many of them were long-time critics of the establishment JACL and all its works. The third group—Japanese Americans who initially had no strong opinions about redress—consisted mainly of people who thought that nothing would come of the movement, that it was just "pie in the sky." As the redress movement gained momentum, however, the overwhelming majority of the community came, in one way or another, to support it. One Nisei I know, a man whose marriage plans were interrupted by Pearl Harbor, and who spent more than two years in confinement, originally opposed redress because he had never taken any kind of government "welfare." But when he realized that the courts had awarded as much as $10,000 in damages to each of thousands of persons who had been wrongly detained for a day or two during one of the anti-Vietnam War demonstrations in Washington, D.C., he reasoned that his time behind barbed wire certainly qualified him for similar compensation.

Initial reactions among the American public at large were also mixed. Many felt, as *The New York Times* put it, that while a wrong clearly had been done to the Japanese Americans— something it had not said in 1942—and an apology was in order, a monetary recompense was inappropriate. Many others felt that an apology was long overdue and that it should be accompanied by some kind of payment. However, a sizable minority, mostly persons old enough to remember Pearl Harbor, were either totally opposed to redress, or felt, as one writer of a letter to the editor put it, that since Japan started the war the Japanese government should make any apologies or payments. There was certainly no clear national consensus for monetary redress in the late 1970s and early 1980s.

The leaders of the redress movement, facing formidable political obstacles, felt the need for an "educational" campaign. The "outsiders"—chiefly, William Hohri and a group of Seattle Japanese Americans—got Representative Mike Lowery, a maverick Washington Democrat, to introduce a bill which provided redress payments of $25,000 to each victim and allowed heirs to collect the payments of the deceased. The "insiders," the JACL Redress Committee leaders and the seven Japanese Americans serving in Congress—the four members of Hawaii's congressional delegation, and Hayakawa, and two representatives from California—devised an effective strategy. Rather than introducing a bill calling for monetary redress—which the Redress Committee and all but Hayakawa favored—they opted for the commission approach mentioned earlier and garnered impressive support for it. Senator Daniel K. Inouye (D-Hawaii) arranged for more than fifty co-sponsors for the bill to establish the Redress Commission—an absolute majority of the Senate— and the almost perfunctory Senate hearings in March 1980 "created a good record," as the subcommittee chair, Senator Henry M. Jackson (D-Wash.), put it. Indicative of how the racial climate of opinion had changed is the fact that Jackson as a young congressman during World War II had been virulently anti-Japanese and had felt then that the government was pampering the Japanese Americans. Among those testifying in favor of the commission bill was Clarence Mitchell of the NAACP, representing the civil-rights coalition, and the majority leader of the House of Representatives, Jim Wright (D-Tex.). The only opposition at the hearing came from redress partisan Hohri, who expressed his strong preference for the Lowery bill, which never received a formal hearing. Hohri, and many others, were put off by the language of the bill. They did not feel that it was necessary to have a time-wasting commission to determine what almost everyone, including the most recent Republican President and the incumbent Jimmy Carter, had already conceded: that a great wrong had been done to the Japanese Americans. In addition, the "outsiders" felt that the JACL-sponsored redress demands were too modest, by far.

The bill establishing the Commission on the Wartime Relocation and Internment of Civilians was enacted by Congress late in 1980 without significant opposition. It called for a seven-person commission whose members were to be appointed by three officials, all Democrats: President Carter named three, and Speaker of the House Thomas P. O'Neill of Massachusetts and president pro tem of the Senate Warren G. Magnuson of Washington named two members each. The commission they appointed largely represented the liberal establishment and consisted of a former Supreme Court Justice, Arthur J. Goldberg; a former cabinet member, Arthur S. Fleming, who had been Secretary of Health, Education and Welfare under President Eisenhower; two former Senators, Edward W. Brooke (R-Mass.), the commission's only black, and Hugh B. Mitchell (D-Wash.); a sitting federal judge, William M. Marutani of Philadelphia, who was the commission's only Japanese American; a sitting member of Congress, Daniel E. Lundgren (R-Calif.); and a former federal bureaucrat, Joan Z. Bernstein, who chaired the commission.

In early 1981, after the commission had been created, Senator Ted Stevens, an Alaska Republican, discovered that some of his Aleut constituents had also been affected by Executive Order 9066. (Aleuts are the Native American inhabitants of the Aleutian chain of islands.) The Japanese invasion of the two westernmost Aleutian Islands in mid-1942 had caused the U.S. Army to evacuate the remaining Aleuts from the rest of their islands because of real military necessity: the army wanted to take them out of harm's way. No question had been raised about their loyalty. Nevertheless, the Aleuts were treated miserably, dumped in unhealthy sites in southern Alaska, and left without even the minimal medical and other social services that the government provided for the incarcerated Japanese Americans. Although no one had Aleuts in mind when Executive Order 9066 had been promulgated in February 1942, the terms of that decree, which were broad enough to fit anyone, were applied to them. When Stevens proposed that a representative of the Aleut people, the Reverend Ishmael Gromoff, a priest of the Russian Orthodox Church, be added to the Redress Commission, the leaders of the redress coalition in the Senate quickly agreed, as this would insure additional support. House Speaker O'Neill, however, insisted that if the Senate, now Republican, got an extra appointment, the House should get one, too. This was agreed to: when the Speaker discovered that the Senate was going to name a priest, he vowed, so the story goes, that he would appoint a priest, too, and named the Jesuit Robert F. Drinan, a liberal Democrat who had been forced to resign from Congress by papal decree and in 1981 headed Americans for Democratic Action. There is no record of what the new President, Ronald W. Reagan, thought when he was asked to sign a commission for one of his staunchest opponents, or if he even noticed that he had done so.

In the winter and spring of 1981, the Redress Commission organized itself, appointed a staff, consulted scholars, and began its investigations. It then held hearings in the nation's capital and in New York, Chicago, Los Angeles, San Francisco, and Seattle. The Washington hearings featured testimony from federal officials who had supervised the wartime incarceration. Almost all, like Edward J. Ennis, who had headed the Aliens Division of the Department of Justice, found some or all of the wartime actions regarding the Japanese Americans regrettable and supported some kind of monetary redress. Abe Fortas, who as Under-secretary of the Interior had the responsibility to oversee the War Relocation Authority (WRA) which ran the camps for Japanese Americans, testified that it was "a tragic error" and that "mass evacuation . . . was never justified."

Two wartime officials, John J. McCloy and Karl R. Bendetsen, were hostile to the claims of Japanese Americans and rejected both the appropriateness of an apology and of monetary redress. McCloy had been Assistant Secretary of War and was the highest-ranking surviving official who had participated in the 1942 decision. After the war, he became U.S. High Commissioner to Germany and one of the so-called wise men, crucial members of the American foreign-policy establishment during the Cold War years. In 1981, McCloy was still vigorously combative, despite his advanced age. He maintained that the wartime actions of the American government were proper and said that he was defending the reputation of Franklin Roosevelt; however, many observers felt that it was his own reputation that he perceived to be at risk. At one point in his testimony, McCloy argued that the wartime indignities heaped on the Japanese American people were proper "retribution" for the attack on Pearl Harbor by the naval and air forces of the Empire of Japan—though he immediately withdrew the word when challenged by Commissioner Goldberg. Bendetsen, who had been a strategically placed middle-echelon army bureaucrat, adopted what some lawyers now call a Nuremberg defense, the defense many Nazi generals used during the war-crimes trials in Germany after World War II. He was just following orders, Bendetsen said, and, in any case, he maintained, what was done to the Japanese Americans wasn't so bad after all.

The most impressive aspect of the Relocation Commission's hearings—which began in the nation's capital and were continued in cities across the country—was the testimony of those who had been incarcerated. Most Japanese Americans had not publicly dwelt on their wartime experiences and in many instances had not even talked about them to their own children. Some of this is related to the well-known "blame the victim" syndrome: the false notion that if something bad happens to a person—kidnapping, rape, disease—it is at least in part the victim's fault. In addition, Japanese American culture taught that individuals should not bring shame or disgrace on the group, and since being put in a concentration camp seemed disgraceful, it was best not to talk about the experience. These cultural attitudes had acted as a dam on the emotions of the victims of the wartime incarceration, effectively blocking their feelings for almost four decades, a phenomenon psychologists call denial. The dam burst and the denial ended during the hearings as the detainees one after the other testified with great passion about what they had endured. Many wept openly, some broke down, and, when at the Los Angeles hearings Senator Hayakawa testified against monetary redress, the audience, largely Japanese American, disrupted the hearing with shouts, boos, and hisses.

In early 1983, the Redress Commission issued its report, *Personal Justice Denied*. Its unanimous and unambiguous findings, based on staff research and what it had learned from the hearings, were consistent with what most scholars had been saying for decades.

The promulgation of Executive Order 9066 was not justified by military necessity, and the decisions which followed from it—detention, ending detention and ending exclusion—were not driven by analysis of military conditions. The broad historical causes which shaped these decisions were race prejudice, war hysteria and a failure of political leadership. Widespread ignorance of Japanese Americans contributed to a policy conceived in haste and executed in an atmosphere of fear and anger at Japan. A grave injustice was done to Americans and resident aliens of Japanese ancestry who, without any individual review or probative evidence against them, were excluded, removed and detained by the United States during World War II.

The report left open the question of what kind of remedies, if any, the Redress Commission would recommend to the Congress. Six months later, in June 1983, it made five recommendations. They called for:

1. A formal apology by Congress.
2. Presidential pardons for persons who had run afoul of the law while resisting the wartime restraints placed upon Japanese Americans.
3. Congressional recommendations to government agencies to restore status and entitlements lost because of wartime injustices. (For example, many Japanese Americans who were serving in the U.S. armed forces received less than honorable discharges in the weeks immediately after Pearl Harbor, which meant that they were not entitled to veterans' benefits.)
4. Congress to establish and fund a special foundation to "sponsor research and public educational activities . . . so that the causes and circumstances of this and similar events may be illuminated."

The most significant and controversial recommendation called for

5. A one-time, tax-free payment of $20,000 to each Japanese American survivor who had been incarcerated because of ethnicity during World War II. (Individual Aleut survivors, who had previously received some compensation, were given $5,000.) Estimates are that perhaps 60,000 of the 120,000 persons detained are still alive; redress payments to Japanese Americans might total $1.2 billion.

One commissioner, Congressman Lundgren, dissented from recommendations 3, 4, and 5, so those recommendations passed 8–1. He felt that no government money should be disbursed and that an apology and pardons were enough. Lundgren's written dissent maintains:

It is inappropriate that present day taxpayers should be held accountable for actions that occurred 40 years ago.

Should we pay monetary redress for the abhorrent practice of slavery or the inhumane treatment of Indians 100 years ago?

As the bill provided redress for survivors only, Lundgren's arguments were a chain of non-sequiturs. Humorist Mark Russell put it nicely, noting that "one congressman is worried that the Chinese will want back pay for building the railroads in the last century. They'll be beefing up security in Washington for another Bonus March by angry Chinese railroad workers."

By mid-1983, the national climate of opinion seemed to be somewhat more favorable to redress than it had been earlier, probably because media coverage had brought before the public the injustices inflicted upon the Japanese Americans. But the Reagan Administration opposed payments. Congressman Lundgren served as the Administration's anti-redress point man on Capitol Hill. In the federal courts, that role was played by the Department of Justice.

Two distinct legal battles were waged over redress. The first stemmed from the archival research of political scientist and attorney Peter Irons, which demonstrated that the executive branch of the government had suppressed evidence and made false statements in its briefs in the so-called Japanese American Cases decided by the Supreme Court in 1943 and 1944. This meant that the government's arguments before the Supreme Court were tainted and it was possible, under an old common law writ of *coram nobis*, to reopen the cases in the federal district courts in which they had originated. Thus, in the mid-1980s, a group of Asian-American lawyers, with Irons's assistance, were able to reopen the relevant cases in San Francisco, Portland, Oregon, and Seattle. The lawyers hoped not only to win their cases but also that at least one of the cases would reach the Supreme Court and enable that body to reconsider its wartime acquiescence in the incarceration. In each instance, the lawyers—who donated their services—gained courtroom victories. There were variations from court to court, but the general result was the same: the convictions were reversed and the indictments quashed.

The federal district judge in the first case to have a rehearing,

Marilyn Hall Patel, handed down a particularly eloquent decision. She said, in voiding the indictment and 1942 conviction of Fred T. Korematsu for failure to report for incarceration:

> *Korematsu* remains on the pages of our legal and political history . . . As historical precedent it stands as a constant caution that in times of war or declared military necessity our institutions must be vigilant in protecting constitutional guarantees. It stands as a caution that in times of distress the shield of military necessity and national security must not be used to protect governmental actions from close scrutiny and accountability. It stands as a caution that in times of international hostility and antagonisms our institutions, legislative, executive and judicial, must be prepared to exercise their authority to protect all citizens from the petty fears and prejudices that are so easily aroused.

The Reagan Administration refused to appeal the lower-court verdicts it lost, thus preventing any rehearing by the highest court. But the court decisions themselves and the publicity they received helped to create a favorable climate of opinion for the legislative consideration of redress. (The Redress Commission took no part in the cases that were outside its mandate.)

The other legal battle had a less happy result. William Hohri and his supporters hired a firm of Washington attorneys to file a class-action suit asking $25.2 billion ($210,000 each for all who were incarcerated, or their heirs) in damages from the federal government as redress for the wrongs done to Japanese Americans during and after World War II. The suit was never really heard. Dismissed by a District of Columbia federal judge in May 1983 on the technical grounds of untimely filing, it was reinstated by the Court of Appeals for the District of Columbia. In this instance, the government was willing to appeal to the highest court, which ruled, without opinion, in June 1987 that the suit was barred by both sovereign immunity and the statute of limitations, and, in addition, had been filed in the wrong federal appellate court. A lower court again dismissed the suit in March 1988, and it lingered in a kind of legal twilight until

October 1988, when the Supreme Court denied the last writ of *certiorari.*

While the legal processes were in progress, the legislative process was stalled. Although clear majorities in each house favored redress, the hostility of the Reagan White House and the constant budget struggles of the 1980s made it impossible to get congressional action until 1988, more than five years after the Redress Commission made its report.

The bill that enacted redress, the Civil Liberties Act of 1988, was dropped into the hopper of the House of Representatives by the majority leader, Tom Foley (D-Wash.), as the first session of the 100th Congress opened in January 1987. It encompassed all five of the CWRIC's recommendations and was given the symbolic number H.R. 442, for the heroic 442nd Regimental Combat Team, the segregated Japanese American unit which had fought so courageously in Italy and France during the war. Eventually, at least 140 other congressmen, twenty of them Republicans, signed on as co-sponsors.

The Reagan Administration's continued opposition to redress became apparent in the House hearings on H.R. 442. An Assistant Attorney General, Richard K. Willard, presented the Administration's line, testifying:

> It may be that the [Redress Commission] is correct in concluding that the assumptions on which the exclusion and detention programs were based were erroneous. It is a long unsubstantiated further step, however, to brand those actions as a product of raqcial prejudice, or hysteria, and a failure of political leadership [sic] . . . Moreover, some of the [CWRIC's] conclusions are suspect. These matters are best left to historical and scholarly analysis rather than debated by Congress.

Willard also attacked the idea of cash payments, insisting that the Japanese American Claims Act of 1948 was "a comprehensive statutory scheme which provided a reasonable and balanced contemporaneous remedy to affected individuals." This was nonsense, as the 1948 act applied just to demonstrated losses of property and only indemnified a small fraction of actual property loss. The whole purpose of the Redress Commission's proposed awards was to recognize the violation of individual civil rights, a subject the Justice Department's spokesman failed to mention.

Most other testimony was favorable. Perhaps most striking was that of the representative of the American Jewish Committee, who endorsed redress and made a telling comparison to the billions of dollars in reparations that the West German government had paid to individual victims of the Holocaust and to the State of Israel as surrogate and heir for those who left no survivors. Several of the Japanese American members of congress told about their own experiences. Norman Mineta (D-Calif.), who was incarcerated as a small child, testified:

> I realize that there are some who say that these payments are inappropriate. Liberty is priceless, they say, and you cannot put a price on freedom. That's an easy statement when you have your freedom. But to say that because constitutional rights are priceless they really have no value at all is to turn the argument on its head. Would I sell my civil and constitutional rights for $20,000? No. But having had those rights ripped away from me, do I think I am entitled to compensation? Absolutely. We are not talking here about the wartime sacrifices that we all made to support and defend our nation. At issue here is the wholesale violation, based on race, of those very legal principles we were fighting to defend.

As expected, the views of the advocates of redress prevailed. The bill passed the House in September 1987 by a vote of 243–141. But there were more than enough no votes to sustain a veto. The no's came chiefly from fiscal conservatives in both parties. An amendment by Representative Lundgren to eliminate monetary redress but make a formal apology to Japanese Americans drew 161 positive votes. The Senate did not act for seven months but in April 1988 passed a similar bill by the apparent veto-proof margin of 69–27. Minor differences between the House and the Senate versions were adjusted by a conference report which passed the Senate without recorded vote on July 27.

Four days later Ronald Reagan, who had not said anything publicly about the issue, sent a letter to Speaker of the House Jim Wright which reversed the position taken by his Administration for the previous five years. The President now endorsed redress and urged its ratification. The reasons for the reversal are not clear, and redress is merely one of many topics that goes unmentioned in Reagan's memoirs. Critics pointed out that 1988 was an election year, a time when politicians are reluctant to offend any interest group. With the threat of a veto removed, the House vote, once thought crucial, became routine. The bill cleared its last legislative hurdle on August 4, when the House passed it 257–159—not enough to override had there been a veto—and the President made it the law of the land in a signing ceremony in the Old Executive Office Building six days later.

Ronald Reagan took center-stage and read his lines as if he had been a long-term supporter of redress. He even replayed —and rewrote—an old scene from 1945 by referring to his cameo role as a "young actor" in a ceremony in which General Joseph W. Stilwell presented a medal to the brother of a Nisei who had been killed fighting with the 442nd in Europe. What the President did not say was that he had been assigned temporary duty as an aide to Stilwell for publicity purposes and that the script had been written by the War Department's publicity people, or by the Office of War Information.

The Civil Rights Act of 1988 enacted into law the recommendations of the Redress Commission. Since payments were to be made only to survivors, persons who had actually been incarcerated, the heirs of those who died before Reagan signed the bill were entitled to nothing. But from August 10, 1988, on, the right to redress was fully vested for all who were still alive then, so the heirs of those who died subsequently could collect. However, no one collected anything at that time. In the American legislative system, authorization and appropriation are two separate matters, and the bill Reagan signed made no appropriations. The only thing that happened in 1988 was that the Department of Justice, which was responsible for finding those eligible for redress payments and certifying them, set up an

Office of Redress Administration and quickly published rules and regulations for redress payments in the Federal Register. And, unlike the Justice Department in administering the 1948 Japanese American Claims Act, the Redress Administration has consistently made fair and even generous rulings.

Congress, still engaged in annual budget struggles with the White House and operating under the restraints of the Gramm–Rudman–Hollings budget law, made no appropriations for redress for more than two years. In late 1989, Senator Inouye, after giving up on a redress appropriation for the fiscal year beginning that October 1, executed an astute tactical maneuver. He got his colleagues to agree to add a clause to a bill appropriating money for the Commerce, State and Justice departments which made redress payments an entitlement program in the ensuing fiscal year (October 1, 1990–September 30, 1991) and thereafter. Entitlement programs, which include such things as social security, are not subject to the restraints of the Gramm–Rudman–Hollings statute. Although some conservatives, notably Jesse Helms (R-N.C.), objected, Inouye's amendment passed, 74–22.

Warren Rudman (R-N.H.), one of the fathers of budget restraint, and an important supporter of making redress an entitlement, stated: "There is a time when one whose name is part of the Deficit Control Act of 1985 believes the Budget Act ought to be waived, and this is one of those times." He urged his colleagues to give "overwhelming support to waive the Budget Act to redress finally for the now elderly [Japanese] Americans, the injustice that money will never recompense."

The House accepted the Senate amendment and President George Bush signed the appropriation bill into law on November 21, 1989, paving the way for redress payments to begin in late 1990. The statute called for the payment of $500 million annually until all eligible persons had been compensated. It was stipulated that payment would begin with the oldest and continue in the order of age.*

---

* Since there were more survivors than the "experts" anticipated, an additional $400 million was appropriated in the Civil Liberties Act Amendments of 1992, signed into law on September 27, 1992. In signing, President George Bush noted that "no monetary payments can fully compensate" Japanese Americans for their suffering.

The first checks were issued on October 9, 1990, more than forty-eight years after the mass incarcerations began. Attorney General Dick Thornburgh conducted a small ceremony at the Justice Department in which he personally presented redress checks to a handful of the oldest survivors, five of whom were a hundred years of age and older. His gracious remarks were a far cry from the long resistance to redress by his predecessors. Praising the redress process and those who had struggled to obtain it, the Attorney General said:

> Your struggle for Redress and the events that led to today are the finest examples of what our country is about, and of what I have pledged to protect and defend, for your efforts have strengthened the nation's Constitution by reaffirming the inalienability of our civil rights.

Americans like to tell themselves that, sooner or later, democracy corrects its own mistakes; redress, it can be argued, is an example of that process. Those who had struggled for redress against what seemed to be very long odds were justified in celebrating their victory. But what had been won? At least half the victims of Executive Order 9066 did not live to see their vindication and collect their checks and the letter of apology from the President. Norman Mineta, Warren Rudman, and the others were right in insisting that no amount of money could redress the injustices of the war years and the decades of waiting that followed. The government's apology was an important precedent, but even as the first redress checks were being distributed, some government agencies were acting as if the Arab American minority in the United States was somehow allied to the Iraqi tyrant Saddam Hussein and therefore a threat to national security.

The achievement of redress was clearly a victory for democracy. Those who fought for it and those who helped bring it to fruition are all entitled to feel proud of a job well, if belatedly, done. But merely to celebrate the event, thus participating in what Richard Hofstadter called "the literature of national self-congratulation," would be as crass as attempting to deny that these brutal acts were ever committed against the Japanese

Americans. This book has tried to explain *how* and *why* the outrage happened. That is the role of the historian and his book, which is to analyze the past. But this historian feels that analyzing the past is not always enough. So, in the epilogue that follows, I will explore the disturbing question of whether such a thing could happen again.

6

COULD IT HAPPEN AGAIN?

THE tragedy of the Japanese Americans is now half a century old. It was a tragedy that betrayed not just the Japanese Americans, but, in the words of Morton Grodzins, "all Americans," because it violated fundamental values of American democracy in the guise of fighting a war to preserve that democracy. It was not the first such violation, nor, alas, the last, but it was the first and so far the only time that the American government has violated, en masse, the rights of an ethnic group, the second- and third-generation Japanese Americans, to which its Constitution had given citizenship. To be sure, worse things have been done in the past. The denial of the human rights of aboriginal peoples and the sometimes genocidal way in which European American settlers deprived them of their land, the enslavement of millions of African Americans and their continued relegation to inferior status even after the end of slavery, are, by any reckoning, great crimes against humanity.

The recovery of the Japanese Americans as a group, in the years after World War II, has been remarkable. By the mid-1960s, just two decades after the last concentration camp closed, a neo-conservative social scientist, William Petersen, then a professor at the Berkeley campus of the University of California, coined the phrase "model minority" to describe the behavior and status of just one minority group: the Japanese Americans. Petersen specifically excluded Chinese Americans and Filipino Americans, along with blacks and Mexican Americans, from that category, describing them as non-achieving minorities. He

used the term "model" in two ways: both to praise the achievements of the Japanese Americans and to suggest that their
success should be emulated by other groups. To Petersen, what
was crucial was that the Japanese American achievement was
accomplished "by their own totally unaided effort." His praise
of the Japanese Americans was used to denigrate the programs
of Lyndon Johnson's Great Society, especially those directed at
helping blacks. "For all the well-meaning programs and countless
scholarly studies now focused on the Negro, we hardly know
how to repair the damage that the slave traders started," he
maintained.

Other social scientists soon appropriated Petersen's term,
stripped it of its conservative ideology, and applied it to Asian
Americans in general. This latter usage caught on, and by 1982
Newsweek headlined a feature story "Asian Americans: A 'Model
Minority.'" The image of the Asian in American society had
clearly changed, and changed more rapidly than cultural norms
usually do. All such group images, sometimes called stereotypes,
must inevitably distort the reality they attempt to describe. What
cannot be denied is that many Asian Americans, beginning with
some Japanese Americans and now including large numbers of
other Asian groups, particularly Chinese, Koreans, and Asian
Indians, have achieved middle-class status in both education
and income. Social change and the transformed images which
go along with it are complex phenomena difficult to categorize
precisely, but surely the factors governing the mutation of the
Asian American image, what Peter I. Rose has labeled the shift
from "pariahs to paragons," include all of the following:

1. An increase in numbers, largely because of immigration. By
   1990, the Census Bureau reported, there were 7.3 million
   Asian Americans, nearly 3 percent of the total population;
   in 1940, Asian Americans constituted but four-tenths of one
   percent (.004) of the population. While this increase had
   some negative results, the less racist climate of opinion in
   the post-1965 years made it largely positive.
2. An improvement in status both in law and in custom. By
   1952, all legal discrimination had been removed from the

statute books; most crucial were the changes that allowed Asian immigrants the same naturalization rights as other groups.

3. The growing international status of Japan. This, too, had some negative overtones—Japan bashing has become popular—but so far has been largely positive.

4. The ethnic revival—real and imagined—in the United States in the 1960s and 1970s, which made ethnicity a positive social attribute.

5. An increase in American cosmopolitanism, which embraced foreign foods, cultures, travel, and even brides (but rarely grooms) from Asian countries.

6. Increased perception and awareness by the majority of other ethnic groups—blacks, Chicanos, Puerto Ricans, and many recent immigrants from the Caribbean and Central America—deemed more threatening to middle-class values than Asian Americans.

Yet, despite all this, despite their obviously improved position and status in American society, many Japanese Americans were less confident than might have been expected after their victory. No one expressed this better than the Canadian historian and activist Ken Adachi, who helped to win the redress battle in Canada. In 1942 he and other Japanese Canadians suffered a fate remarkably similar to that of their American cousins and achieved a comparable redress agreement with the Canadian government in 1988, shortly after the American law was enacted. Adachi's immediate reaction was:

> Of course I feel better today, as a Canadian, than I did last week. But it doesn't quite assuage my anger. No, not quite. I cannot summon up tears. Our individual and collective experience lies too deep for a facile display of emotions and easy rhetoric.

Among the factors that dampened the celebration of the Japanese Americans in 1988, and later, in 1990, when the first checks were issued, were the long delay, the fact that so many of the detainees were no longer alive to see their vindication, and, perhaps more than anything else, the nagging question whether, given the circumstances, it could happen again: could the government seize them or some other group in the face of a national emergency, real or imagined?

In the more desperate days of the Cold War, when school-children were drilled to hide under desks as part of the "precautions" against atomic attack, it seemed likely that if any group were going to be incarcerated en masse, it would be ideological rather than ethnic "enemies" of the republic. There was even a statute on the books for twenty-one years which spelled out the precise terms under which incarceration could take place. That law was the Emergency Detention Act of 1950, Title II of the Internal Security Act of that year, approved overwhelmingly over President Truman's veto. The detention act was consciously modeled on the procedures used to put away the Japanese Americans, because those procedures had been sanctioned as constitutional by the Supreme Court.

The act itself was fairly simple. After twelve turgid paragraphs about the dangers of a "world-wide Communist organization" using "treachery, deceit, infiltration . . . espionage, sabotage, terrorism and any other means deemed necessary, to establish a Communist totalitarian dictatorship," a thirteenth paragraph stated that "the world Communist movement" presented

a clear and present danger to the security of the United States . . . and make it necessary that Congress enact appropriate legislation . . . designed to prevent [the world-wide Communist conspiracy] from accomplishing its purpose in the United States.

To do this, Congress authorized:

(14) The detention of persons who there is reasonable grounds to believe probably will commit or conspire with others to commit espionage or sabotage is, in a time of internal security emergency, essential to the common defense and to the safety and security of the territory, the people and the Constitution of the United States.

The next two sections of the law set up the mechanism by which this was to be accomplished. Section 102 provided that in the event of any one of three occurrences—the invasion of the United States or any of its possessions, a declaration of war by Congress, or an insurrection within the United States in aid of a foreign enemy—the President was authorized to proclaim an internal security emergency which would continue until terminated either by another Presidential proclamation or by a concurrent resolution of both Houses of Congress. Section 103 provided:

> Whenever there shall be in existence such an emergency, the President, acting through the Attorney General, is hereby authorized to apprehend and by order detain, pursuant to the provisions of this title, each person as to whom there is reasonable ground to believe that such person probably will engage in, or probably will conspire with others to engage in, act of espionage or of sabotage . . .

The parallels with the Japanese American incarceration are unmistakable. The President issues an order and authorizes a cabinet member to lock up persons regarded as suspicious. As was the case under Executive Order 9066, no overt act was necessary, merely the judgment of an unelected official. The only difference was the substitution of the Attorney General for the Secretary of War. Provisions were made for individual hearings, but these were to take place *after* incarceration, not before. Realizing that in 1942 there had been a delay of several months before enough camps were ready, the law ordered the Justice Department to keep such places in readiness. And the Department found it convenient to reactivate Tule Lake as one of the standby camps.*

Happily, the detention law was never applied. Those who complain that the war in Vietnam was undeclared might ponder what might have happened to war protesters had Lyndon

---

* Another standby camp was located at Allenwood, Pennsylvania. It was eventually reconverted by the Bureau of Prisons into a minimum-security facility for non-violent prisoners. Former Attorney General John N. Mitchell served his sentence there for Watergate crimes.

Johnson or Richard Nixon been able to use a formal state of war as a pretext for declaring an internal security emergency. The law was finally repealed by Congress in 1971, with the reluctant consent of the Justice Department. Deputy Attorney General Richard G. Kleindienst informed Congress in late 1969 that, since many Americans believed that the law might "one day be used to accomplish the apprehension and detention of citizens who hold unpopular beliefs," and that "various groups, of which our Japanese American citizens are most prominent, look upon the legislation as permitting a reoccurrence of the roundups which resulted in the detention of Americans of Japanese ancestry during World War II," the Department believed that the psychic benefit to be gained from "repeal of this legislation . . . outweighs any potential advantage which the act may provide in a time of internal security emergency." Everyone concerned with civil liberties in America was delighted that the Emergency Detention Act was no longer the law of the land, but the Japanese Americans were quick to point out that they had been shipped off to camps in 1942 even without such a law.

We now know that the Nixon Administration considered all sorts of "antidotes" to mass disaffection, many of them illegal or extralegal, but it did not, apparently, seriously consider mass incarceration. Subsequent Administrations have been relatively restrained, but, of course, there has been no national crisis of the magnitude of Pearl Harbor, and the Cold War has been winding down so steadily that it is difficult even for diehard cold warriors to remain wrought up by the threat of "the international Communist conspiracy." However, the last three Administrations—those of Carter, Reagan, and Bush—seem to have considered some kind of mass incarceration of persons associated with some foreign country during a crisis involving that country.

The Carter Administration, at the time of the takeover of the United States Embassy in Teheran, took preliminary steps against Iranians—mostly college students—living in the United States. When the Immigration and Naturalization Service's filing system proved so chaotic that it could not provide the White House with approximate numbers or names and addresses, the

Administration asked American colleges and universities to provide them, and most complied to the best of their ability. Precisely what the government's intentions were is not clear; in the event, no mass incarceration resulted.

During the Reagan Administration, the treatment of illegal Haitian immigrants, the so-called Caribbean boat people, including their detention in Miami's notorious Krome Avenue camp, was eventually moderated by a federal judiciary not constrained by a war situation. (Partly to avoid both federal courts and immigration lawyers, the Bush Administration set up a camp for later Haitian refugees inside the American military base at Guantanamo Bay, Cuba.) The excursions and alarms of the Reagan years, including Presidential fulminations against the possible influx of great masses of "feet people," remained largely rhetorical. To be sure, there were no large-scale foreign crises for the Administration to deal with.

Just before and during the brief hostilities in the Persian Gulf in 1990–91, some agents of the Bush Administration interrogated Arab American leaders, both citizen and alien. When representatives of those communities and civil-liberties organizations protested, the interrogations ceased, and the government made the lame excuse that the federal agents were just trying to protect those they had interrogated. And there was sporadic violence against Arab Americans.

These post-World War II events, when weighed against the Japanese American incarceration, do not add up to very much and many apologists for the Administrations involved would say that even to mention them in connection with the massive violations of civil rights by the Roosevelt Administration is inappropriate. But they were violations of the spirit of the Constitution and posed a real threat to the groups and individuals concerned. They did happen, even in a society in which both racial discrimination and xenophobia have been greatly reduced. What they might have developed into had they been accompanied by a tangible threat to national security, the kind of disaster that occurred at Pearl Harbor, is, of course, impossible to say. They do demonstrate, however, an American propensity to react against "foreigners" in the United States during times of external crisis, especially when those "foreigners" have dark skins. Despite great improvement in American race relations, there are still huge inequities between whites and non-whites, and potentially explosive emotions exist among both the oppressed and their oppressors. While most optimists would argue that, in America, concentration camps are a thing of the past— and one hopes that they are—many Japanese Americans, the only group of citizens ever incarcerated simply because of their genes, would argue that what has happened before can surely happen again.

7

EPILOGUE: SINCE 1990

EVENTS since September 11, 2001, might suggest to some that the note on which the first edition of this book ended was prophetic. However, things are not that simple. And before any parallels can be considered, the statutory and administrative evolution of the payments to Japanese American survivors must be taken into account. At this writing, March 2004, the last War Relocation Authority camp for Japanese Americans closed fifty-eight years ago, while the last redress payment occurred only five years ago; the relevance of the Japanese American experience during World War II is not only to events of yesteryear but also, in a historical sense, to those of only yesterday.

The redress process turned out to be more expensive than Congress or the presidential Commission on Wartime Relocation and Internment of Civilians (CWRIC) had estimated. In September 1992 Congress passed without much fuss important amendments to the 1988 Civil Liberties Act. These not only appropriated an additional $400 million, bringing the total to $1.65 billion, but also contained a "Benefit of the Doubt" clause providing that any applicant for redress should be considered eligible in narrowly disputed cases. The first President Bush signed the law (P.L. 102–371) on September 22, 1992, some five weeks before election day. His signing statement concluded:

No monetary payments can ever fully compensate loyal Japanese Americans for one of the darkest incidents in

American constitutional history. We must do everything possible to ensure that such a grave wrong is never repeated.

Thus, unlike the case of the 1948 Japanese American Claims Act in which the Department of Justice (DoJ) made every effort to minimize claims, its newly set-up Office of Redress Administration (ORA) was clearly proactive in its efforts to make as many awards as possible within the statute as amended. It not only advertised for claimants but asked historians and archivists to help it settle some claims. Under what it called "constructive relocation" it authorized compensation for Japanese American railroad workers in the Southwest who were fired but never incarcerated, and for Japanese American farmers in Hawaii who were ordered off their land by the Army but remained at liberty.

The payments for redress continued into the Clinton administration, and he signed the last redress letters. The redress books were closed for Japanese American victims in February 1999, more than ten years after passage of the original act. The ORA reported that 82,210 claims had been paid to Japanese Americans, 22,210 above the original estimate of 60,000. In addition, the Justice Department settled a class action suit brought in 1996 by five Japanese from Latin America who were among more than 2,000 Japanese brought into the United States and interned in camps run by the INS in the Southwest. In June 1998 nearly 600 still in the United States received $5,000 each and a letter of apology. None of the 4,058 Germans and 288 Italians similarly brought to the United States from fifteen Latin American countries has received any payment.

The attention given redress over more than a decade not surprisingly increased national awareness of what is usually but improperly called Japanese American internment despite the passage of more than half a century since the event. The difference between "internment" and a more proper term such as "incarceration" is, in the final analysis, the difference between the rule of law and the doctrine that, if you declare an "emergency"—in this case termed a "military necessity"—then the rule of law no longer applies.

Responding to that enhanced awareness, both Congress and recent presidents have provided funding for long-standing plans by the National Park Service to memorialize what happened to Japanese Americans during World War II. On March 3, 1992, Bush the elder signed Public Law 102–248, making the remains of the concentration camp at Manzanar a National Historic Site. Several previous attempts to do this had failed to gain congressional approval. As the site closest to Los Angeles, home to the continent's largest concentration of Japanese Americans, it was a natural for further development, which was slow to come. In 1996, as part of an Omnibus Public Lands Act, the site was enlarged, and the federal budget of fiscal 2001 contained a $5.1 million appropriation for construction. Finally, on April 24, 2004, the Park Service was able to open a visitors' center with newly constructed exhibits and some restoration of vestiges of the original camp.

Earlier, on November 9, 2000, a small park near the Capitol in Washington was dedicated as a memorial to both the 120,000 Japanese Americans who were incarcerated and the 26,000 who served in the Army during World War II. As is customary in Washington for smaller memorials, the National Capital Planning Commission approved it, and the government donated the land, but a private group, in this instance a committee of Japanese Americans, raised the necessary funds. The park features a fifteen-foot sculpture of two cranes—one struggling to fly through barbed wire and the other soaring above it—a bell tower, a rock garden, and cherry trees.

Although then President Bill Clinton did not attend the ceremony—Attorney General Janet Reno and Secretary of Commerce Norman Mineta, the first Japanese American to serve in the cabinet, did—later that day Clinton announced that he had directed the Secretary of the Interior to develop recommendations to preserve existing internment sites and provide for their public interpretation. "This nation must never forget," he announced, "the difficult lessons of the Japanese American internment camps during World War II, and the inspirational lessons of patriotism in the face of that injustice."

On January 17, 2001, three days before the end of his term, Clinton used authority granted under the Antiquities Act of

1906 (34 *Stat.* 225)—which had been a key piece of Theodore Roosevelt's conservation reform program—to proclaim the camp called Minidoka, in Idaho, a National Monument and ordered the Secretary of the Interior to have the National Park Service prepare plans to manage and interpret the site.

As had been the case at Manzanar, there was some local protest. The Twin Falls *Times News* editorialized that Clinton had "miss[ed] the mark on all fronts."

All too often, revisionist historians foment conspiracy theories and suggest sinister motivations for events of long ago. Rounding up Japanese-American residents along the West Coast and sending them to relocation camps at the start of World War II smacks of racism now—but back then it was a matter of national security . . .

Has America atoned for unilaterally relocating these citizens? We think so. Remember, every surviving person who spent time in a relocation camp has already received financial compensation from the United States government.

But the state's leading newspaper, the *Idaho Statesman,* reported that the "plan appears to be well-received in Jerome County," where Minidoka was located, and quoted its congressman, Michael K. Simpson, a Republican who had just been elected to his second term:

I don't think there's really any opposition to it. I'd rather it be done through legislation rather than using the Antiquities Act, but this is the kind of thing the act was designed to do.

President Clinton left office without acting on any of the other eight relocation centers in California, Arizona, Utah, Wyoming, Colorado, and Arkansas, which have benefited from only minimal historical preservation efforts by state, local, and private bodies. (See Map 2, page 56.) The only other federally directed activity has been the Bainbridge Island Japanese-American memorial Study Act of 2002 (P.L. 107–363), which directed the Secretary of the Interior to conduct a study of the dock area from which the 227 Japanese American residents of the island, the first group to be "relocated," had been taken away for shipment to Manzanar. Part of the stated rationale was that while both Manzanar and Minidoka were in remote areas, Bainbridge Island, a short ferry ride from Seattle, was easily accessible.

Major historical events, such as the experiences of Japanese Americans during World War II, have aftershocks that continue to be felt for decades. That will also be true of the terrorist atrocity that we have learned to call 9/11, which destroyed New York's World Trade Center towers, seriously damaged the Pentagon in Washington, and killed some 3,000 persons, including those who perished on the four hijacked airliners.

Historical analogies are always tricky, particularly when one of the things being compared is a current event. Contemporary history is, after all, a contradiction in terms. Nevertheless, some differences and similarities can be readily seen. In 1941–42, as the CWRIC noted, the root causes of the incarceration of Japanese Americans were "race prejudice, war hysteria and a failure of political leadership." In 2001 race prejudice—accentuated by religious prejudice—and hysteria were clearly present, but at the highest levels of government there were repeated warnings not to make assumptions about guilt based on race or religion. Yet it must be noted that subsequent governmental and private actions often flew in the face of those warnings. Immigration officials applied different standards to "Middle Eastern" aliens who were in technical violation of certain regulations while ignoring the same violations when committed by other aliens. Airport inspectors often focused on physical appearance rather than on evidence or legal status when subjecting passengers to special searches.

Moreover, governmentally regulated airlines have forced individuals—citizens and aliens—who look like the "enemy" to leave flights for which they had tickets, sometimes winning praise for doing so. "I was relieved at the story of the plane passengers a few weeks ago who refused to board if some Mideastern-looking guys were allowed to board," wrote Peggy Noonan, a *Wall Street Journal* contributing editor. "I think we're going to require a lot of patience from a lot of innocent people. . . . And you know, I don't think that's asking too much." Even more disturbing than such blathering is the fact that the cabinet officer responsible for aviation, Secretary of Transportation Norman Mineta—himself a child victim of wartime incarceration, and who often recounts going off to a 1942 Assembly Center in his Cub Scout uniform—made no public criticism of such blatant discrimination.

A striking difference is that while in 1942 almost no public figures spoke out against the massive violations of the rights of citizens, in the aftermath of 9/11 there was much public criticism of significantly lesser governmental violation of rights. And the analogy with the Japanese American experience was raised so often that it seems obvious that the increased awareness of that gross injustice was a factor in the heightened sensitivity within and without the government.

Clearly, when compared with what was done to Japanese Americans during World War II, government actions after September 11 do not seem, at first glance, to amount to very much. Indeed, many media commentators have objected that even to mention them in connection with the massive violations of civil liberties by the Roosevelt administration is inappropriate.

That conclusion is an evasion: the kind of evasion that has allowed Americans to offer apologies for actions previously taken against a group once perceived to be outsiders, and then do the same thing to a different group. Time and again, scholars (if not the government) have noted that the nation has often violated the spirit of the Constitution. Time and again further violations have been made, usually against a different group under different circumstances.

Optimists assure us that a mass incarceration of American citizens in concentration camps will not recur and point to the relative mildness of the governmental reaction after 9/11 as evidence of that. But reflection on our past suggests we ought not to be so sanguine. We must remember that it was not just the disaster at Pearl Harbor but the subsequent sequence of Japanese triumphs that triggered Executive Order 9066 seventy-four days later. Shouldn't we then ask, if terrorist attacks on

American soil had continued after September 11, would the current government reaction have been so moderate? And were there to be a recurrence of such attacks, would there not be those in our security establishment who would argue that the moderation after 9/11 was a contributing factor in the renewed assaults?

AN ESSAY IN
PHOTOGRAPHS

The photographs that follow attempt to recapitulate, roughly in chronological order, the sequence of events that most of the Japanese American people went through in the aftermath of Pearl Harbor, from the nervous weeks of waiting, through incarceration in assembly and relocation centers, to their eventual release for school or work. The final three images depict some of the contemporary ripples still being created by the wartime events.

Civilian Exclusion Order No. 5

WESTERN DEFENSE COMMAND AND FOURTH ARMY
WARTIME CIVIL CONTROL ADMINISTRATION
Presidio of San Francisco, California
April 1, 1942

INSTRUCTIONS
TO ALL PERSONS OF
JAPANESE
ANCESTRY
LIVING IN THE FOLLOWING AREA:

All that portion of the City and County of San Francisco, State of California, lying generally west of the north-south line established by Junipero Serra Boulevard, Worchester Avenue, and Nineteenth Avenue, and lying generally north of the east-west line established by California Street, to the intersection of Market Street, and thence on Market Street to San Francisco Bay.

All Japanese persons, both alien and non-alien, will be evacuated from the above designated area by 12:00 o'clock noon, Tuesday, April 7, 1942.

No Japanese person will be permitted to enter or leave the above described area after 8:00 a. m., Thursday, April 2, 1942, without obtaining special permission from the Provost Marshal at the Civil Control Station located at:

1701 Van Ness Avenue
San Francisco, California

The Civil Control Station is equipped to assist the Japanese population affected by this evacuation in the following ways:

1. Give advice and instructions on the evacuation.

2. Provide services with respect to the management, leasing, sale, storage or other disposition of most kinds of property including: real estate, business and professional equipment, buildings, household goods, boats, automobiles, livestock, etc.

3. Provide temporary residence elsewhere for all Japanese in family groups.

4. Transport persons and a limited amount of clothing and equipment to their new residence, as specified below.

Reprinted by: Japanese American Citizens League
National Committee to Repeal the Emergency Detention Act
c/o Ray Okamura
1150 Park Hills Road, Berkeley, Calif. 94708

(OVER)

OBSERVED:

referably the head of
f the property is held,
to the Civil Control
ust be done between
42, or between 8:00

e for the Reception

ch member of the

;

ly;

, bowls and cups for each

essential personal effects for each member of the family.

All items carried will be securely packaged, tied and plainly marked with the name of the owner and numbered in accordance with instructions received at the Civil Control Station.

The size and number of packages is limited to that which can be carried by the individual or family group.

No contraband items as described in paragraph 6, Public Proclamation No. 3, Headquarters Western Defense Command and Fourth Army, dated March 24, 1942, will be carried.

3. The United States Government through its agencies will provide for the storage at the sole risk of the owner of the more substantial household items, such as iceboxes, washing machines, pianos and other heavy furniture. Cooking utensils and other small items will be accepted if crated, packed and plainly marked with the name and address of the owner. Only one name and address will be used by a given family.

4. Each family, and individual living alone, will be furnished transportation to the Reception Center. Private means of transportation will not be utilized. All instructions pertaining to the movement will be obtained at the Civil Control Station.

Go to the Civil Control Station at 1701 Van Ness Avenue, San Francisco, California, between 8:00 a. m. and 5:00 p. m., Thursday, April 2, 1942, or between 8:00 a. m. and 5:00 p. m., Friday, April 3, 1942, to receive further instructions.

J. L. DeWITT
Lieutenant General, U. S. Army
Commanding

See Civilian Exclusion Order No. 5

Some of the first group of Japanese Americans to be evacuated from San Francisco waiting at 2020 Van Ness Avenue for buses to take them to an assembly center, April 6, 1942. The man on the right, facing the camera, is Mike Masaoka   WRA PHOTOGRAPH BY DOROTHEA LANGE

(opposite)
Civilian Exclusion Orders, such as this one for an area in San Francisco, were posted on telephone poles and in store windows in Japanese American neighborhoods, usually six days before the residents were scheduled to be "relocated" COURTESY JAPANESE AMERICAN CITIZENS LEAGUE

Issei mother. A Japan-born woman and her American-born children in Hayward, California, waiting for a bus to take them to an assembly center, May 8, 1942   WRA PHOTOGRAPH BY DOROTHEA LANGE

(opposite, top)
Prisoners from San Pedro arriving under guard at Santa Anita Assembly Center, April 5, 1942   WRA PHOTO BY CLEM ALBERS

(opposite, bottom)
Family living quarters, Tanforan Assembly Center, San Bruno, California, April 29, 1942. Each door of these former horse stalls leads into a family unit of two rooms; the rear rooms have neither a door nor windows   WRA PHOTOGRAPH BY DOROTHEA LANGE

American prisoners at the Heart Mountain Relocation Center in Wyoming. The buildings at right are typical barrack-type residences

WRA PHOTOGRAPH

(opposite, top)
The relocation center at Jerome, Arkansas, November 17, 1942

WRA PHOTOGRAPH BY TOM PARKER

(opposite, bottom)
Mess halls, like this one at the Jerome (Arkansas) camp, provided monotonous settings for monotonous food

WRA PHOTOGRAPH BY TOM PARKER

These three former California college students, George John Furutani (Manzanar), Sukio Oji (Gila River), and Joe Nishimura (Manzanar), were enrolled at the University of Nebraska by the fall semester of 1942   WRA PHOTOGRAPH BY TOM PARKER

The WRA hired some of the prisoners after they were released from camp. These nine young women, Fukako Sei (Minidoka), Joan Ishiyama (Heart Mountain), Ryo Kayama (Tule Lake), Kiyoko Magai (Jerome), Marvel Maeda (Poston), Katherine Kagayama (Topaz), Sashi Amaku (Gila River), Jane Oi (Granada), and Sally Tsusimoto (Manzanar), all worked for the agency in Washington in the fall of 1943

WRA PHOTOGRAPH BY GRETCHEN VAN TASSEL

Some prisoners, like engineering graduate Eugene Y. Komo, went from camp to defense plants. Komo supervised the making of 20 mm anti-aircraft shells at Chicago's Superior Type Company

Joseph Gerald Osamu Sakamoto and Mary Ann Tsuchi Sakamoto, both aged eighty, celebrating their golden wedding anniversary in the camp at Minidoka, December 11, 1943. The couple had come to America in 1894; Mr. Sakamoto had run a furniture store and a vegetable market in Seattle   WRA PHOTOGRAPH

These prisoners had mixed feelings about Visitors' Day at their nursery school in the camp at Jerome, Arkansas, March 10, 1943

WRA PHOTOGRAPH BY TOM PARKER

This house, at 2820 Winslow Avenue, Cincinnati, served as an American Friends Service Committee hostel for several hundred Japanese Americans who resettled there

WRA PHOTOGRAPH BY HENRY IWAI, JANUARY 28, 1944

Fred Korematsu, whose incarceration was upheld by the U.S. Supreme Court in December 1944, and whose conviction was voided in the first of the *coram nobis* cases in October 1983, receives the Presidential Medal of Freedom from President Bill Clinton. The President said, in part: "In the long history of our country's constant search for justice, some names of ordinary citizens stand for millions of souls: Plessy. Brown. Parks. To that distinguished list, today we add the name of Fred Korematsu"   WHITE HOUSE PHOTOGRAPH

WWII CONFLICTS IN THE SOUTH PACIFIC ARE WELL DOCUMENTED. THE ONES IN SOUTH ARKANSAS HAVE BEEN SOMEWHAT NEGLECTED.

In 1942, wartime hysteria swept the nation, prompting the U.S. government to incarcerate over 100,000 innocent Japanese Americans living on the west coast and in Hawaii. Over 16,000 of those people ended up at camps in two desolate south Arkansas towns – Rowher and Jerome. Life Interrupted is dedicated to helping us learn from this history. And to keep us from repeating it. For more information, visit www.lifeinterrupted.org.

INTERRUPTED
The Japanese American Experience in WW II Arkansas

www.lifeinterrupted.org

This poster was part of a large 2004 project, "Life Interrupted: The Japanese American Experience in WW II Arkansas," which documented the WRA Camps at Jerome and Rohwer and the people who lived in them   LIFE INTERRUPTED, A PARTNERSHIP BETWEEN
THE UNIVERSITY OF ARKANSAS AT LITTLE ROCK PUBLIC
HISTORY PROGRAM AND THE JAPANESE AMERICAN NATIONAL
MUSEUM WITH MAJOR FUNDING PROVIDED
BY THE WINTHROP ROCKEFELLER FOUNDATION

This Manzanar graveyard marker was refurbished by the National Park Service for the 2004 opening of the National Historic Site. Its characters may be translated: "Monument to console the souls of the dead." On the back (unseen here) it says: "Erected by Manzanar Japanese, August 1943"   NATIONAL PARK SERVICE PHOTOGRAPH AND TRANSLATION

Suggestions for
Further Reading

There is a large literature on the wartime ordeal of the Japanese American people; the following is a representative selection. General treatments include: Alan R. Bosworth, *America's Concentration Camps* (NY, 1967); Audrie Girdner and Anne Loftis, *The Great Betrayal* (NY, 1969); Roger Daniels, *Concentration Camps, USA* (NY, 1972), revised as *Concentration Camps, North America* (Melbourne, Fla., 1981); Michi Weglyn, *Years of Infamy* (NY, 1976); and Roger Daniels, *Asian America* (Seattle, 1988).

Important specialized studies include: Donald E. Collins, *Native American Aliens* (Westport, Conn., 1985), which studies those who renounced their citizenship and their struggle to regain it; John Dower, *War Without Mercy* (NY, 1986), which dissects the racism of World War II on both sides of the Pacific; Peter Irons, *Justice at War* (NY, 1983), which examines the role of the Department of Justice and the courts; Thomas James, *Exile Within* (Cambridge, Mass., 1987), which analyzes the educational system created in the camps; Harry H. L. Kitano, *Japanese Americans* (Englewood Cliffs, NJ, 2nd ed., 1976), an account of the Japanese American people by a social psychologist; and Gary Y. Okihiro, *Cane Fires* (Philadelphia, 1991), which studies the different treatment accorded the Japanese of Hawaii.

Two books, Valerie J. Matsumoto, *Farming the Home Place: A Japanese American Community in California, 1919–1982* (Ithaca, 1993), and Sandra C. Taylor, *Jewel of the Desert: Japanese American Internment at Topaz* (Berkeley, 1993), study groups of rural and urban Japanese Californians before, during, and after the wartime experience.

Two books that examine the parallel process in Canada are

Ken Adachi, *The Enemy That Never Was*, 2nd ed. (Toronto, 1991), and Ann G. Sunahara, *The Politics of Racism* (Toronto, 1981). C. Harvey Gardiner, *Pawns in a Triangle of Hate* (Seattle, 1981) tells of the fate of the Peruvian Japanese.

On the question of redress, the official report of the Commission on Wartime Relocation and Internment of Civilians, *Personal Justice Denied* (Washington, D.C., 1982), is indispensable. An anthology, Roger Daniels, Sandra C. Taylor, and Harry H. L. Kitano, *Japanese Americans: From Relocation to Redress*, 2nd ed. (Seattle, 1991), has material on redress and the postwar effects of the whole experience. William M. Hohri, *Repairing America* (Pullman, 1988) is a personal account of the redress movement by a participant.

There are several collections of documentary materials, the largest of which are Roger Daniels, ed., *American Concentration Camps: A Documentary History of the Relocation and Incarceration of Japanese Americans, 1941–1945*, 9 vols. (NY, 1989), and a microfilm edition of the *Papers of the Commission on Wartime Relocation and Internment of Civilians*, published by University Publications of America (Frederick, Md., 1984). Arthur A. Hansen, ed., *Japanese American WW II Evacuation History Project*, 5 vols. (Westport, Conn., 1990–2) is a wide-ranging collection of oral histories. The Library of Congress has microfilmed all the newsletters and papers from the assembly and relocation centers.

Since the first edition of this work, the literature has swelled considerably: only a few books can be noted here. Most useful to students is Alice Yang Murray, ed., *What Did the Internment of Japanese Americans Mean?* (New York, 2000), which includes a historiographical essay by Murray and an anthology presenting various points of view. Significant monographic additions to the literature include two works that explore and analyze the struggles of Japanese American college students: Gary Y. Okihiro, *Storied Lives: Japanese American Students and World War II* (Seattle, 1999), which focuses on the ways in which individual students were affected, while Allan W. Austin, *From Concentration Camp to Campus: Japanese American Students and World War II* (Urbana, 2004) examines the efforts of liberal activists to place students and get the government to change its policies. Yoon K. Pak,

Wherever I Go I Will Always Be a Loyal American: Seattle's Japanese American Schoolchildren During World War II (New York, 2001) and Karen L. Riley, *Schools Behind Barbed Wire: The Untold Story of Wartime Internment and the Children of Arrested Enemy Aliens* (Lanham, Md., 2001) treat the educational experiences of incarcerated pupils. David K. Yoo, *Growing Up Nisei: Race, Generation, and Culture Among Japanese Americans of California, 1924–1949* (Urbana, 2000) examines the lives of young adults.

Louis Fiset, *Imprisoned Apart: The World War II Correspondence of an Issei Couple* (Seattle, 1997) explains how one Issei couple was separated by the government, which interned the husband in Montana and sent the wife to a WRA camp in Idaho. Life in a WRA camp is described in Richard S. Nishimoto, *Inside an American Concentration Camp: Japanese American Resistance at Poston, Arizona*, selected and edited, with an introduction and afterword, by Lane Ryo Hirabayashi (Tucson, 1995). Seiichi Higashide, a Japanese Peruvian, describes his imprisonment in both Peru and the United States in *Adios to Tears: The Memoirs of a Japanese-Peruvian Internee in U.S. Concentration Camps* (Seattle, 2000). Max Paul Friedman, *Nazis and Good Neighbors: The United States Campaign Against the Germans of Latin America in World War II* (New York, 2003) explains the program that brought alien enemies from Latin America to the United States for internment.

The major contributions to legal history are Eric L. Muller, *Free to Die for Their Country: The Story of the Japanese American Draft Resisters in World War II* (Chicago, 2001), which examines trials of draft resisters, and Harry N. and Jane L. Scheiber, "Bayonets in Paradise: A Half-Century Retrospect on Martial Law in Hawaii, 1941–1946," *University of Hawai'i Law Review* 19, no. 2 (1997): 478–648, which provides a detailed and definitive account of how the army ruled civilians.

Mitchell T. Maki, Harry H. L. Kitano, and S. Megan Berthold, *Achieving the Impossible Dream: How Japanese Americans Obtained Redress* (Urbana, 1999) makes a detailed analysis of the organized campaign for redress. Three books elaborated aspects of Japanese American military history: Stanley L. Falk and Warren M. Tsuneishi, eds., *American Patriots: MIS in the War Against Japan* (Vienna, Va., 1995) relates the contributions of

Japanese Americans in Army military intelligence; Brenda L. Moore, *Serving Our Country: Japanese American Women in the Military during World War II* (New Brunswick, N.J., 2003) tells about Nisei in the Women's Army Corps; Franklin Odo, *No Sword to Bury: Japanese Americans in Hawai'i During World War II* (Philadelphia, 2004) explains how Japanese American soldiers defended Hawaii after Pearl Harbor and later served in Europe. Klancy Clark de Nevers, *The Colonel and the Pacifist: Karl R. Bendetsen, Perry H. Saito, and the Incarceration of Japanese Americans During World War II* (Salt Lake City, 2004) contains a devastating portrait of Bendetsen.

Finally, two revisionist works challenged what Alice Yang Murray calls the "master narrative" of wartime incarceration, which this book accepts. Greg Robinson, *By Order of the President: FDR and the Internment of Japanese Americans* (Cambridge, Mass., 2001) argues that FDR was the mover rather than the moved, while Tetsuden Kashima, *Judgment Without Trial: Japanese American Imprisonment During World War II* (Seattle, 2003) contends that rather than being a result of wartime stress, the mass incarceration was long planned.

The following are a collection of Web sites likely to be permanent and, unlike many Web sites on this topic, accurate.

Japanese American National Museum
http://www.janm.org/main.html
This is the premier site for Japanese American history.

Smithsonian's National Museum of American History
"A More Perfect Union: Japanese Americans and the U.S. Constitution"
http://americanhistory.si.edu/perfectunion/experience/
An exhibit created for the bicentennial of the Constitution.

National Park Service
The War Relocation Camps of the World War II: When Fear Was Stronger Than Justice
http://www.cr.nps.gov/NR/twhp/wwwlps/lessons/
89manzanar/89manzanar.htm
In lesson-plan form with links to individual camps.

Truman Presidential Museum and Library
The War Relocation Authority and the Incarceration of
Japanese-Americans during WW II
http://www.trumanlibrary.org/whistlestop/study_collections/
japanese_internment/background.htm
Includes historical documents.

The Bancroft Library, the University of California at Berkeley
War Relocation Authority Photographs of Japanese-American
Evacuation and Resettlement, 1942–1945
http://www.oac.cdlib.org/findaid/ark:/13030/tf596nb4ho
Nearly 7,000 images of "publicity pictures" taken by government photographers, which attempt to put the best possible
face on the camps, often showing smiling inmates.

The University of Arkansas–Little Rock
Life Interrupted: The Japanese American Experience in WW II
Arkansas
http://www.lifeinterrupted.org
An online version of a multi-museum group of exhibits opened
in the fall of 2004.

The Densho Educational Web Site
http://www.desho.org
Densho, a Seattle-based nonprofit organization, produces les-
son plans, often document-based, about the Japanese American
experience.

APPENDIX

DOCUMENT 1

EXECUTIVE ORDER NO. 9066

The President

EXECUTIVE ORDER

AUTHORIZING THE SECRETARY OF WAR TO PRESCRIBE MILITARY AREAS

WHEREAS the successful prosecution of the war requires every possible protection against espionage and against sabotage to national-defense material, national-defense premises, and national-defense utilities as defined in Section 4, Act of April 20, 1918, 40 Stat. 533, as amended by the Act of November 30, 1940, 54 Stat. 1220, and the Act of August 21, 1941, 55 Stat. 655 (U.S.C., Title 50, Sec. 104);

NOW, THEREFORE, by virtue of the authority vested in me as President of the United States, and Commander in Chief of the Army and Navy, I hereby authorize and direct the Secretary of War, and the Military Commanders whom he may from time to time designate, whenever he or any designated Commander deems such action necessary or desirable, to prescribe military areas in such places and of such extent as he or the appropriate Military Commander may determine, from which any or all persons may be excluded, and with respect to which, the right of any person to enter, remain in, or leave shall be subject to whatever restrictions the Secretary of War or the appropriate Military Commander may impose in his discretion. The Secretary of War is hereby authorized to provide for residents of any such area who are excluded therefrom, such transportation, food, shelter, and other accommodations as may be necessary, in the judgment of the Secretary of War or the said Military Commander, and until other arrangements are made, to accomplish the purpose of this order. The designation of military areas in any region or locality shall supersede designations of prohibited and restricted areas by the Attorney General under the Proclamations of December 7 and 8, 1941,[1] and shall supersede the responsibility and authority of the Attorney General under the said Proclamations in respect of such prohibited and restricted areas.

I hereby further authorize and direct the Secretary of War and the said Military Commanders to take such other steps as he or the appropriate Military Commander may deem advisable to enforce compliance with the restrictions applicable to each Military area hereinabove authorized to be designated, including the use of Federal troops and other Federal Agencies, with authority to accept assistance of state and local agencies.

I hereby further authorize and direct all Executive Departments, independent establishments and other Federal Agencies, to assist the Secretary of War or the said Military Commanders in carrying out this Executive Order, including the furnishing of medical aid, hospitalization, food, clothing, transportation, use of land, shelter, and other supplies, equipment, utilities, facilities, and services.

This order shall not be construed as modifying or limiting in any way the authority heretofore granted under Executive Order No. 8972,[2] dated December 12, 1941, nor shall it be construed as limiting or modifying the duty and responsibility of the Federal Bureau of Investigation, with respect to the investigation of alleged acts of sabotage or the duty and responsibility of the Attorney General and the Department of Justice under the Proclamations of December 7 and 8, 1941, prescribing regulations for the conduct and control of alien enemies, except as such duty and responsibility is superseded by the designation of military areas hereunder.

FRANKLIN D. ROOSEVELT
THE WHITE HOUSE,
February 19, 1942.

[No. 9066]

[F. R. Doc. 42–1563; Filed, February 21, 1942; 12:51 p.m.]
[1] 6 F.R. 6321, 6323, 6324.
[2] 6 F.R. 6420. Source: *Federal Register*, Vol. 7, No. 38, p. 1407 (Feb. 25, 1942)

DOCUMENT 2
TABLE OF WRA CAMP POPULATION, 1942–1946

Center	Location		Date first evacuee arrived	Peak Population		Date last resident departed
	State	County		Date	Population	
Central Utah	Utah	Millard	9-11-42	3-17-43	8,130	10-31-45
Colorado River	Arizona	Yuma	5- 8-42	9- 2-42	17,814	11-28-45
Gila River	Arizona	Pinal	7-20-42	12-30-42	13,348	11-10-45
Granada	Colorado	Prowers	8-27-42	2- 1-43	7,318	10-15-45
Heart Mountain	Wyoming	Park	8-12-42	1- 1-43	10,767	11-10-45
Jerome	Arkansas	Drew & Chicot	10- 6-42	2-11-43	8,497	6-30-44
Manzanar	California	Inyo	¹6- 1-42	9-22-42	10,046	11-21-45
Minidoka	Idaho	Jerome	8-10-42	3- 1-43	9,397	10-28-45
Rohwer	Arkansas	Desha	9-18-42	3-11-43	8,475	11-30-45
Tule Lake	California	Modoc	5-27-42	12-25-44	18,789	3-20-46

¹ Center under jurisdiction of WCCA until June 1, 1942.

Source: Adapted from U.S. Department of the Interior, *WRA: A Story of Human Conservation* (Washington, D.C., 1946), Table 1, p. 197

DOCUMENT 3
PROCLAMATION 4417

PROCLAMATION 4417
AN AMERICAN PROMISE
By the President of the United States of America

A PROCLAMATION

In this Bicentennial Year, we are commemorating the anniversary dates of many of the great events in American history. An honest reckoning, however, must include a recognition of our national mistakes as well as our national achievements. Learning from our mistakes is not pleasant, but as a great philosopher once admonished, we must do so if we want to avoid repeating them.

February 19th is the anniversary of a sad day in American history. It was on that date in 1942, in the midst of the response to the hostilities that began on December 7, 1941, that Executive Order No. 9066 was issued, subsequently enforced by the criminal penalties of a statute enacted March 21, 1942, resulting in the uprooting of loyal Americans. Over one hundred thousand persons of Japanese ancestry were removed from their homes, detained in special camps, and eventually relocated.

The tremendous effort by the War Relocation Authority and concerned Americans for the welfare of these Japanese-Americans may add perspective to that story, but it does not erase the setback to fundamental American principles. Fortunately, the Japanese-American community in Hawaii was spared the indignities suffered by those on our mainland.

We now know what we should have known then—not only was that evacuation wrong, but Japanese-Americans were and are loyal Americans. On the battlefield and at home, Japanese-Americans—names like Hamada, Mitsumori, Marimoto, Noguchi, Yamasaki, Kido, Munemori and Miyamura—have been and continue to be written in our history for the sacrifices and the contributions they have made to the well-being and security of this, our common Nation.

Source: *Federal Register*, Vol. 41, No. 35 (Feb. 20, 1976)

The Executive order that was issued on February 19, 1942, was for the sole purpose of prosecuting the war with the Axis Powers, and ceased to be effective with the end of those hostilities. Because there was no formal statement of its termination, however, there is concern among many Japanese-Americans that there may yet be some life in that obsolete document. I think it appropriate, in this our Bicentennial Year, to remove all doubt on that matter, and to make clear our commitment in the future.

NOW, THEREFORE, I, GERALD R. FORD, President of the United States of America, do hereby proclaim that all the authority conferred by Executive Order No. 9066 terminated upon the issuance of Proclamation No. 2714, which formally proclaimed the cessation of the hostilities of World War II on December 31, 1946.

I call upon the American people to affirm with me this American Promise—that we have learned from the tragedy of that long-ago experience forever to treasure liberty and justice for each individual American, and resolve that this kind of action shall never again be repeated.

IN WITNESS WHEREOF, I have hereunto set my hand this nineteenth day of February in the year of our Lord nineteen hundred seventy-six, and of the Independence of the United States of America the two hundredth.

GERALD R. FORD

INDEX

aboriginal peoples, discrimination against, 107
Adachi, Ken, quoted, 109
African Americans: enslavement of, 4; discrimination against, 6, 107; segregation in military, 35; not model minority, 107–8
Aleuts, and EO 9066, 95
Alien Land Acts, California: (1913), 14–15; (1920), 14; end of, 88–9
Alien Registration Act (1940), 24
Aliens Division, Department of Justice: list of aliens to be interned, 24; conflicts with War Department, 32–3; denaturalization policy, 84–5
Allenwood, Pennsylvania, prison, 111
American Civil Liberties Union: withdraws from Hirabayashi case, 59; opposes draft resisters, 64
American Federation of Labor, anti-Asian, 10
American Friends Service Committee: organizes college student resettlement, 73; hostels for resettlers, 78
American Jewish Committee, supports redress, 102
American Legion, anti-Japanese activities, 82
anti-Chinese movement, 6–7, 11–12
anti-Japanese movement, 8–15, 17, 41, 75, 88–9, 90
Antiquities Act of 1906, 117–8
Arab Americans, discrimination against, 105, 113, 119–20
Arkansas–Little Rock, University of, Public History Program poster, 136
Army Language School: moved to Minnesota, 76; in San Francisco, 75–6; utilizes Japanese Americans, 76–7
Arrington, Leonard, cited, 75
Arthur, Chester A., signs exclusion act, 7
Asian immigrants, history of, 4, 108
Asian Indians, 108; naturalization of, 88